YOU ARE SECURE

A I M E E
J O S E P H

DEVOTIONS FOR WHEN LIFE IS UNCERTAIN

New Growth Press, Greensboro, NC 27401
newgrowthpress.com
Copyright © 2024 by Aimee Joseph

Cover Design: Alecia Sharp
Interior Design and Typesetting: Alecia Sharp

ISBN: 978-1-64507-427-4 (Print)
ISBN: 978-1-64507-428-1 (E-book)

Library of Congress Cataloging-in-Publication Data

Names: Joseph, Aimee, 1983- author.
Title: You are secure : devotions for when life is
uncertain / Aimee Joseph.
Description: Greensboro, NC : New Growth Press,
[2024] | Series: Gospel truth for women | Includes
bibliographical references.
Identifiers: LCCN 2023050442 (print) | LCCN
2023050443 (ebook) | ISBN 9781645074274
(print) | ISBN 9781645074281 (ebook)
Subjects: LCSH: Anxiety--Religious
aspects--Christianity. | Uncertainty--Religious
aspects--Christianity. | Hope--Religious
aspects--Christianity. | Bible--Devotional
literature.
Classification: LCC BT731.5 .J67 2024 (print) |
LCC BT731.5 (ebook) | DDC 242/.4--dc23/
eng/20240220
LC record available at https://lccn.loc.gov/2023050442
LC ebook record available at https://lccn.loc.
gov/2023050443

Printed in India

31 30 29 28 27 26 25 24   1 2 3 4 5

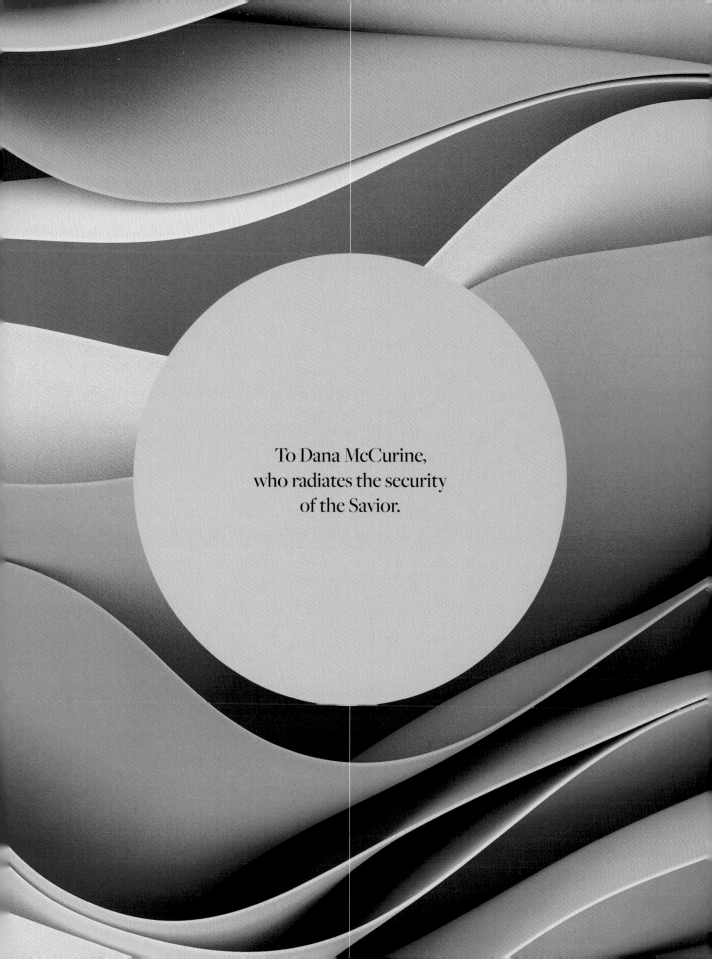

To Dana McCurine,
who radiates the security
of the Savior.

CONTENTS

INTRODUCTION

OUR SENSE OF SECURITY is only as stable as the object of our hope. If we find security in our finances, we will ride the roller coaster of Wall Street. If we find confidence and identity in our marriage, our joy and peace will fluctuate with every fight or moment of miscommunication. If we draw our security from a political party, we will be elated when that party is in power and devastated with every election loss. We very quickly find that peace is elusive when it's attached to anything that is constantly changing.

We may be tempted to think that feelings of instability and insecurity are mostly modern problems related to globalization, industrialization, and technology; however, these are ancient problems that have plagued the human heart and marked the human experience for thousands of years. We have always been trying to answer the question: Where does security come from?

The early church in Colossae was being challenged by this question—in what were they going to base their hope and confidence? The apostle Paul was deeply concerned for the young believers of this city—a church planted by Epaphras out of the beloved church in Ephesus with whom he was deeply familiar. He wrote this short but soaring letter to address the specific ways that the Colossians' stability was being jeopardized by clever lies and the infiltration of false beliefs. Paul prayed and longed for them to hold firm to the hope of the gospel as he reminded them that they had all they needed in Jesus Christ.

While this is a short epistle (the fancy word for a New Testament letter), it is jam-packed with rich truths about God that directly apply to our lives today. I read it when I first became a believer in high school and have not stopped studying it since. Every time I go through its words, I am more and more astounded by the reality it loudly proclaims: Christ in you, the hope of glory (Colossians 1:27).

Paul composed this message during his imprisonment in Rome. During the same time, he also wrote his letter to the church in Ephesus—thus there are many parallel ideas and passages between the two letters, as you will see throughout our devotional study. Paul felt the weight of actual shackles, but he also felt the weight of the well-being of the young churches that he had helped pioneer and plant.

As you will soon find out for yourself, this letter is all about the incredible reality of union with Christ. In our present culture which is identity-obsessed, Paul's words have much to say to our deepest identity. Amidst a largely insecure world, our security is anchored into the unchanging person of Jesus. Even though the Colossians lived thousands of years before us in a different culture, we share with them this same need for a reminder of our unchanging hope. Though many things have changed since Paul wrote this letter to the early church, the needs and fears of the human heart have not.

When we anchor our souls and lives in Jesus Christ, who is the same today and yesterday and forever, we begin to experience the peace and security God always intended for us (Hebrews 13:8). Yet if you are like me, it is a daily battle to remember my true identity and not be swept away by the lie of finding hope and rest in anything other than Jesus.

I am so expectant of what God will do in and through us as we dig into the book of Colossians to learn about the sufficiency of Christ and our unshakeable security in him.

Identity is a buzzword in our culture. We are being told that we can create our own sense of self, but this means that we must constantly curate and maintain our fragile sense of self. Christ offers believers a much better invitation to find our completeness in him! An identity founded on Christ provides the unshakeable security we long for.

OUR TRUE IDENTITY

OUR DEEPEST IDENTITY

IDENTIFY

○ How does our culture define identity?

○ What are some of your identifiers?

● I AM A WIFE, a mother, a writer, a church member, a daughter, a San Diegan, and a lover of books, among other things. While these realities are true of me, they are not my deepest identity.

In our culture, we often conflate our *identifiers* (job, marital status, life stage, accomplishments) with our *identity* (our sense of who we are). When we do so, we run the risk of missing the grace and peace that flow from knowing our deepest identity, which is found in belonging to Christ.

When Paul introduced himself, there were scores of things he could have said about himself. After all, he was a learned Jewish scholar, trained under one of Judaism's sharpest minds. He was an unbelievable speaker with honed rhetoric and had been grouped with the brightest and best of Jewish leaders. He was unmatched in his zeal for God (Acts 22:3–5; Philippians 3:4–7). Instead of recalling any of these claims to fame, however, Paul introduced

PAUL, AN APOSTLE OF CHRIST JESUS BY THE WILL OF GOD, AND TIMOTHY OUR BROTHER, TO THE SAINTS AND FAITHFUL BROTHERS IN COLOSSAE: GRACE TO YOU AND PEACE FROM GOD OUR FATHER

COLOSSIANS 1:1-2

himself simply as "an apostle of Christ Jesus by the will of God" (Colossians 1:1).

Paul's pedigree was not his deepest identity; his relationship to Christ defined him most deeply. In his letter to the Philippians, Paul gives us a window into the source of his confidence: "I count everything as loss because of the surpassing worth of knowing Christ Jesus my Lord" (Philippians 3:8). In another letter, Paul tells us that his identity comes neither from others' views of him nor his own view of himself (1 Corinthians 4:3–4). Paul most deeply defined himself as who God says that he was: a beloved, adopted son and servant (Galatians 4:4–7).

If our identities are founded upon our identifiers, we will live insecure and unstable lives. We will be overly inflated when we are performing well and overly deflated when we are underperforming. The first step toward lasting stability is to stand upon who we are in Christ. As our roots grow deeper into who we are in Jesus, we will be able to say with Paul, "But by the grace of God I am what I am, and his grace toward me was not in vain" (1 Corinthians 15:10).

CONSIDER

- Where are you tempted to allow your identifiers to overshadow your true identity in Christ?

- What past sins, struggles, lies, or failures keep you from believing that your deepest identity is as a saint before God?

- Read 1 Peter 2:9–10. What do these verses say about our deepest identity as believers?

GOSPEL FRIENDSHIPS

IDENTIFY

○ Who knows you well?

○ Do you have friends who speak into your life and are unafraid to point you to your deepest identity?

W H E N it comes to remembering your identity in Christ, do you ever feel like you have amnesia? I cannot tell you how many times I will read a verse in my time alone with God in the morning, reminding me of my secure status and security through Christ, only to completely live like I have forgotten it by lunchtime. The apostle Paul understood our tendency to forget the deepest truths about ourselves. Paul's interactions with the early church and with those he mentored personally tell us that we are not alone in our spiritual forgetfulness and that we need others speaking into our lives on a consistent basis to remind us of what is true.

In today's Scripture passage, we see Paul speaking into and strengthening the gospel identity of Timothy, one of his closest friends and ministry partners. When it came to personality, Paul and Timothy could not have been more different. We know from the book of Acts and Paul's personal testimonies that he was a

I THANK GOD WHOM I SERVE, AS DID MY ANCESTORS, WITH A CLEAR CONSCIENCE, AS I REMEMBER YOU CONSTANTLY IN MY PRAYERS NIGHT AND DAY. AS I REMEMBER YOUR TEARS, I LONG TO SEE YOU, THAT I MAY BE FILLED WITH JOY.

2 TIMOTHY 1:3-4

naturally confident, driven leader. We also know from the letters Paul wrote to Timothy and their interactions that Timothy was prone to insecurity, fear, and anxiety. Their friendship and partnership centered on their shared identity as believers in Christ and their shared purpose in advancing the gospel.

As he wrote to Timothy from prison, awaiting impending death, Paul takes the time to remind Timothy of who he really is in Christ. There were many important things Paul wanted to say in his last words to his best friend, but before he speaks about ministry instructions or warnings, he begins by reaffirming Timothy's deepest identity.

Paul knew the stories of Timothy's upbringing and early influences (2 Timothy 1:5; 3:14–15). He knew Timothy's present temptations and fears (1 Timothy 1:18–19). He also spoke into Timothy's future, reminding him of who God was making him into (2 Timothy 1:13–14). Even after years of preaching the gospel alongside Paul, Timothy needed to be reminded of who he was and would be in Christ.

Paul knew how quickly we forget the depth and riches of our identities in Christ. He knew the power of the enemy's lies and twisted truths (John 8:44). He knew the human heart's struggle to believe and live out of the love of Christ. Thus, he took the time to remind his friends who they really were in Christ.

We are prone to forget our deep identity. We are prone to try to do the Christian life alone. We, like the early church, need to be reminded of who we are (or more accurately, of *whose* we are). We need friends who know the places we hide, the lies that lodge deep within us, and the longing we have to be more like Christ. We need extra sets of eyes to help us notice God's gracious hand in our daily lives. When we forget the glorious reality of our identity in Christ, we need friends who help us remember!

CONSIDER

- What do we learn about Paul and Timothy's relationship from these verses?

- Where do you see tendencies in your own life to try to do the Christian life alone?

- What lies challenge the truth of your identity in Christ?

- Who has God brought into your path that might be a potential partner in life and ministry?

NAME   NOTES

IDENTIFIED BY FAITH, HOPE, + LOVE

IDENTIFY

○ What words would you use to describe yourself?

○ What themes most mark your life as a believer?

 FAITH, HOPE, AND LOVE are three shop-worn words in our culture. They are used so often and so broadly that when we hear them in the Scriptures, we tend to gloss over them quickly, assuming we know what they mean. In today's verses, Paul affirms the faith, hope, and love he sees being lived out among the Colossian church.

Biblical faith is central to the Christian life. In fact, faith is the currency of the kingdom of God. The writer of Hebrews gives us his own working definition of faith: faith is the assurance of things hoped for, the conviction of things unseen (Hebrews 11:1). He goes on to say that "without faith it is impossible to please him, for whoever would draw near to God must believe that he exists and that he rewards those who seek him" (v. 6).

We are all putting faith in something or someone. As silly as it sounds, we put faith in those who made our cars when we step into them each morning to head to work or school. We put faith

BELIEVE

WE ALWAYS THANK GOD, THE FATHER OF OUR LORD JESUS CHRIST, WHEN WE PRAY FOR YOU, SINCE WE HEARD OF YOUR FAITH IN CHRIST JESUS AND OF THE LOVE THAT YOU HAVE FOR ALL THE SAINTS, BECAUSE OF THE HOPE LAID UP FOR YOU IN HEAVEN.

COLOSSIANS 1:3–5

in engineers all the time (something I try to not think about when I get on an airplane or an elevator). On a more significant level, we put faith in someone or something for meaning in our lives. Even atheists are putting great faith in their own personal valuation of the universe and the reason for human existence.

Biblical faith is leaning the weight of our whole lives onto the person of Christ who is the visible image of the invisible God (Colossians 1:15).

When we have faith in Christ, we begin to take hold of the hope we have in him and through him. Our faith allows us to hold our present earthly life more loosely because we

know that we have eternal days reserved for us in heaven. Our faith offers a cord of hope we can hold as we walk through suffering, because we know that one day there will be no more pain, sadness, or death (Revelation 21:1–4). The more we are assured of the hope kept for us in heaven and the love lavished on us through Christ, the more we will be empowered to love those around us with a spacious, abundant love (1 Peter 1:3–5).

When Paul writes to the Colossians, he highlights their increasing faith, hope, and love. Can those around us say the same of us?

BIBLICAL FAITH

IS LEANING THE

WEIGHT OF OUR

WHOLE LIVES

ONTO THE PERSON

OF CHRIST WHO

IS THE VISIBLE

IMAGE OF THE

INVISIBLE GOD.

CONSIDER

● What connection does
Paul make between faith
and hope? Between hope
and love?

▨▨▨▨▨

● How often do you think
about the hope laid up
for you in heaven? What
keeps you from consider-
ing our everlasting hope?

▨▨▨▨▨

● Read 1 John 4:13–21.
What do we learn about
love in this passage?

▨▨▨▨▨

● Where do you see "love
gaps" in your life and
relationships? Who are
you struggling to love
currently?

▨▨▨▨▨

DEEP + WIDE

IDENTIFY

○ How did the gospel come to you?

○ How has it moved through you?

WHEN MY BOYS WERE YOUNG, I would volunteer at Vacation Bible School (side note: you don't know tired until you have experienced VBS tired). Since I did not grow up in the church, I was as excited as my children to learn the songs and the stories. I remember singing "Deep and Wide," as we exaggerated our arm movements and dance moves.

While the song was talking about the fountain of God's love, the same exuberant, active descriptions could be said for the scope of the gospel. The gospel was never intended to be a static, inert tidbit of information. Rather, the gospel has always been and always will be dynamic—in motion. It moves wide geographically even as it also transforms us in the depths of our being.

The deeper the gospel digs into our hearts and lives, the more we, like the early disciples, "cannot but speak of what we have seen and heard" (Acts 4:20). As our awareness of our own sin and inability deepens, our dependence upon God and our clinging to

OF THIS YOU HAVE HEARD BEFORE IN THE WORD OF THE TRUTH, THE GOSPEL, WHICH HAS COME TO YOU, AS INDEED IN THE WHOLE WORLD IT IS BEARING FRUIT AND INCREAS-ING—AS IT ALSO DOES AMONG YOU, SINCE THE DAY YOU HEARD IT AND UNDERSTOOD THE GRACE OF GOD IN TRUTH.

COLOSSIANS 1:5b-6

As soon as the Holy Spirit, the Third Person of the Trinity, descended upon the disciples, the gospel began to move both deep and wide. The reality of the gospel changed the disciples from a group of scared men into an unstoppable band. The same gospel that pierced them to the heart powerfully spread from Jerusalem to Judea to Samaria to the outermost parts of the earth (Acts 1:8).

The gospel changes us. It moves *toward* us, takes deep root *within* us, and then begins to move *through* us to the world. As the good news of our security in Christ takes root in our own lives, we will begin bearing fruit that helps the watching world see the power of God. When we begin to realize that our identity and security are not based on our performance, but on the finished work of Jesus Christ, we are able to offer stability and security in an insecure world.

Many people think of the gospel as the ABCs of the Christian life, but in reality, the gospel is the A to Z of the Christian life. The same gospel that saves us continually sanctifies. This is why the apostle Paul told Timothy, "Be strengthened by the grace that is in Christ Jesus" (2 Timothy 2:1) as part of his last words to his mentee. The writer of Hebrews says something similar to the Jewish believers: "It is good for the heart to be strengthened by grace" (Hebrews 13:9).

the gospel deepen as well. The deeper our roots go, the further our branches can grow. The more the gospel transforms us, the more likely we are to share its incredibly good news with those in our spheres of influence.

- Where in these verses do you see the powerful effects of the gospel?

- Read Romans 10:14–17. According to these verses, how does the gospel spread?

- Where have you seen the gospel bearing fruit in your life and increasing in the outside world around you?

- Read 1 Thessalonians 1:4 and 9–10. What are the marks of those who have truly heard and received the gospel?

IT TAKES A VILLAGE

IDENTIFY

○ Who first introduced you to Christ?

○ Who continues to faithfully remind you of your security in Christ?

● SIR ISAAC NEWTON, the famous scientist, humbly said, "If I have seen further, it is by standing on the shoulders of giants." None of us get where we are without a thousand deposits, both small and large, from those around us. When it comes to the Christian life, Christ has done all the saving work; however, he has seen fit that salvation would come from hearing and hearing by the word of God (Romans 10:17). This means that God uses other people in our lives not only to declare the gospel to us initially, but also to point us back to him repeatedly. It really does take a village.

The apostle Paul, who wrote most of the New Testament and pioneered many of the early churches through his missionary journeys, did not do the Christian life alone.

Merely days after his conversion, God used Ananias to restore Paul's sight and to welcome him as a brother even though he had been an outspoken enemy and persecutor of the church (Acts

. . . JUST AS YOU LEARNED IT FROM EPAPHRAS, OUR BELOVED FELLOW SERVANT. HE IS A FAITHFUL MINISTER OF CHRIST ON YOUR BEHALF AND HAS MADE KNOWN TO US YOUR LOVE IN THE SPIRIT.

COLOSSIANS 1:7-8

9:10–19). From early on in his missionary efforts, Paul brought along a band of fellow ministers. While we are most familiar with Barnabas and Timothy, the beginnings and ends of Paul's letters to the churches reveal scores of names of gospel partners.

In fact, Jesus himself sent out his disciples in pairs on their first ministry endeavors. Just as God had declared at the dawn of humanity, "It is not good that the man should be alone" (Genesis 2:18) we still need each other. Just as we needed to hear the gospel from mouth to ear, we continue to need to hear the gospel from the lips of brothers and sisters. When the New Testament writers describe the church, they do so in communal terms:

living stones being built into a spiritual house and one body with many members (2 Peter 2:4–5; 1 Corinthians 12:12–27).

We need other people to speak truth over us, not only when we initially come to know Christ, but also as we seek to walk with him daily. When insecurities surface and when we get tangled in lies, we need others to help buttress and fortify our identities in Christ. When we can't see ourselves rightly, we need another set of eyes to remind us of who we are in Christ.

CONSIDER

- Read ahead to Colossians 4:12–13. In these verses about Epaphras, what else can we learn about our role in the body of Christ?

- What friends or mentors have acted as "faithful ministers of Christ" on your behalf? How did they strengthen your faith?

- Who in your life needs encouragement from the gospel today? What specific actions might you take toward that end?

TAKE + SHARE

Our world is exhausted from working so hard to make, maintain, and validate our own identities. As a believer in Christ, you have been freed from an achieved identity and have been given a received identity. Your confidence and security are not based on your performance, giftedness, or circumstances. When insecurities pop up in your life, take them as opportunities to remind yourself of your unshakeable identity in Jesus. Preach the gospel to yourself and those around you by saying with Paul, "[My] life is hidden with Christ in God" (Colossians 3:3)! Look for opportunities to tell others about the security they can have in Christ.

Prayer is to the Christian life what breathing is to the body. There is no way to know and experience security in Christ apart from a vibrant prayer life. This week, we will explore Paul's prayers for the early church in order to strengthen our own prayer lives!

PRAYERS FOR GOD'S PEOPLE

THE CONTENT OF OUR PRAYERS

IDENTIFY

○ When you pray, what do you ask God to do in your life and in the lives of those you love?

○ What prayer requests do you find yourself offering to God most often?

● DO YOU EVER FIND your mind blank when you sit down to pray for yourself or others? When I finally make space for prayer for my friends and family, I am often confronted by a great blank space in my heart and mind. Where do I even begin?

When I was pregnant with our first son, it would be an understatement to say I was overwhelmed. I was inundated. There were so many things to consider and so many unknowns. When I was in this state, someone approached me and asked if I had begun praying daily for my son's future college roommates and spouse. My jaw literally dropped. Of course, I wanted to be a prayerful mom, but I could barely get through each day.

Amidst such overwhelm, I found great solace in the prayers of Paul. With all the wisdom of a spiritual grandfather, Paul kept things in perspective. He prayed large, sweeping prayers over the churches, even those he had not met, like the church at Colossae. He didn't focus so much on externals; rather, he prayed fervently

AND SO, FROM THE DAY WE HEARD, WE HAVE NOT CEASED TO PRAY FOR YOU, ASKING THAT YOU MAY BE FILLED WITH THE KNOWLEDGE OF HIS WILL IN ALL SPIRITUAL WISDOM AND UNDERSTANDING, SO AS TO WALK IN A MANNER WORTHY OF THE LORD, FULLY PLEASING TO HIM, BEARING FRUIT IN EVERY GOOD WORK AND INCREASING IN THE KNOWLEDGE OF GOD.

COLOSSIANS 1:9–10

and persistently for the condition of their faith and their character. He prayed that they would know the height, depth, and width of the love of God (Ephesians 3:18). He prayed that they would know the comfort of Christ in the middle of their afflictions (2 Corinthians 1:3–4). He prayed that they would walk in unity with one another (Ephesians 4:1–3).

Paul absolutely cared about his spiritual children and grandchildren; however, most of the time, he did not get bogged down in the details or the externals. He longed that they would become more closely conformed to Christ. He begged God that they would see the glories of the gospel increasingly for the rest of their days on earth. He trusted that God would sovereignly steer the details and externals according to the kind intentions of his will (Romans 8:28).

Our prayers reveal the deepest longings of our hearts. Paul's prayers exposed his deep hunger for people to be fully satisfied and secure in Jesus. If I am honest, my prayers often reveal that I am fixated on myself or my loved ones rather than the person of Christ. By modeling our prayers after Christ and the letters of the New Testament, we can begin to pray with power for the people of God!

● What does Paul pray for
this church he has never
even met?

● How do you pray for
the people you love?
(i.e., generically or
specifically? Regularly
or intermittently? Half-
hearted or with passion?)

● What Scriptures can you
begin praying for your
loved ones?

● Read Hebrews 7:25.
What does this verse say
about Christ's
intercession for you?

PRAYERS FOR TRANSFORMATION

IDENTIFY

○ How would you define the word *transformation*?

○ What images come to mind when you think of being transformed?

● DO YOU EVER FEEL dissonance between God's promises to transform his people and your actual experience of said transformation? Does it ever feel like painfully slow work to you?

When our boys were younger, we jumped on the butterfly bandwagon and purchased a kit to watch a caterpillar's metamorphosis into a beautiful butterfly. Every morning (and after every nap), they would excitedly run to press their faces against the little mesh cage only to be frustrated and disappointed. They assumed, as most of us do, that radical change happens quickly. While they eventually celebrated the release of our butterfly, it took more patience than they expected—and patience did not come with the packaging.

The apostle Paul understood that spiritual growth took time in the life of a believer. He continually prayed that believers would stay the course and trust the slow, steady work of God. As we read yesterday, he begged God that the Colossians would grow

I APPEAL TO YOU THEREFORE, BROTHERS, BY THE MERCIES OF GOD, TO PRESENT YOUR BODIES AS A LIVING SACRIFICE, HOLY AND ACCEPTABLE TO GOD, WHICH IS YOUR SPIRITUAL WORSHIP. DO NOT BE CONFORMED TO THIS WORLD, BUT BE TRANSFORMED BY THE RENEWAL OF YOUR MIND, THAT BY TESTING YOU MAY DISCERN WHAT IS THE WILL OF GOD, WHAT IS GOOD AND ACCEPTABLE AND PERFECT.

ROMANS 12:1-2

in wisdom and maturity (Colossians 1:9–10). He also begged believers to do their part by being conformed to Christ rather than the culture around them (Romans 12:2).

Paul prayed for nothing less than full transformation in the lives of the saints. He knew that the same God who began a good work in them would complete it (Philippians 1:6). He also admonished believers to continually treasure Christ. After all, we are most shaped by what we see, experience, and treasure. As Jesus said to his disciples, "Where your treasure is, there your heart will be also" (Matthew 6:21). Paul invites us to be gradually transformed as we daily treasure Christ and feed on his life-giving words to us. We will only be transformed as our minds are renewed. Our minds will only be renewed insofar as we set ourselves before the Word of God.

It may be slow work, but God's work of transformation is always worth both the waiting and the working!

CONSIDER

- What do these verses say about spiritual transformation?

- Where do you feel pressure to conform to the world and its values?

- Paul says that renewal begins in our minds. What thoughts run on repeat through your mind daily? Are they lies from the enemy or truths from the Lover of your soul?

PRAYERS FOR ENDURANCE

IDENTIFY

○ Where do you feel powerless in your life presently?

○ What comes to mind when you think of God's power?

● I DON'T KNOW ABOUT YOU, but when I think of God's power, my mind quickly runs to stories like David and Goliath, the parting of the Red Sea, or Daniel in the lions' den. While these stories most assuredly show off the power of God, God's power shows up in many ways, some of which we wouldn't expect (and often don't really want, if we are honest).

As Paul continues his prayer for the Colossians, he begins to use some power-packed words and phrases. He prays that they would be "strengthened [*dunamoumenoi*] with all power [*dunamei*], according to his glorious might [*kratos*]" (Colossians 1:11).

When I start hearing those words with all their building power and momentum, I begin to expect some miraculous feat of strength or amazing display of power. But Paul's prayers don't move in that direction. He prays that God would give them all that power "for all endurance and patience with joy" (1:11).

I find myself much more inclined to pray for powerful miracles than for power to endure and long suffer under hardship. However, Christ modeled such an application of God's power when "for the joy that was set before him [he] endured the cross" (Hebrews 12:2). Staying the course by remaining in the places and roles God has apportioned for us, however exciting or bland they may be, takes a far greater exertion of strength than a dramatic single display of power.

God strengthens and empowers us, placing his *dunamis* (from which we get the word dynamite) in us that we might stay the course, living lives worthy of the callings we have received. In addition to the power to endure, the apostle Paul highlights God's provision of joy (1:11). The apostle Peter mentions a similar joy when writing to a group of suffering believers: "Though you have not seen him, you love him. Though you do not now see him, you believe in him and rejoice with joy that is inexpressible and filled with glory" (1 Peter 1:8).

Whatever circumstances God ordains for us, he will empower us to endure them with joy. He may not heal the cancer, but he will powerfully sustain as we fight it. He may not remove a difficult challenge, but he will always give us strength to walk upon high places (Habakkuk 3:17–19). As we learn about powerful prayers for the people of God, let's remember to pray with Paul for strength to

[MAY YOU BE] STRENGTHENED WITH ALL POWER, ACCORDING TO HIS GLORIOUS MIGHT, FOR ALL ENDURANCE AND PATIENCE WITH JOY; GIVING THANKS TO THE FATHER, WHO HAS QUALIFIED YOU TO SHARE IN THE INHERITANCE OF THE SAINTS IN LIGHT.

COLOSSIANS 1:11–12

suffer well. Even in the middle of trials and tears, God's comforting presence with us enables not only endurance but also rejoicing (Romans 5:3–5). By God's grace, we will learn to say with the psalmist, "Weeping may tarry for the night, but joy comes with the morning" (Psalm 30:5b).

GOD STRENGTHENS AND EMPOWERS US, PLACING HIS DUNAMIS IN US THAT WE MIGHT STAY THE COURSE, LIVING LIVES WORTHY OF THE CALLINGS WE HAVE RECEIVED.

CONSIDER

- How does Paul describe endurance as a believer?

- Where do you need God's strength to endure in this season of your life?

- Read 2 Corinthians 12:9 where Paul talks about his weakness and God's strength. What resonates with you? Why?

PRAYERS PIERCED WITH LIGHT

IDENTIFY

○ Do you remember how it felt to walk in darkness?

○ How would you describe the feeling of living in the light of Christ?

○ How often do you remember what God has done in your life?

DO YOU EVER FIND YOURSELF utterly over-whelmed by the darkness and brokenness surrounding you? It's not hard to find daily reminders of the depravity and desperate need of humanity. Our news feeds give us reports in real time of destruction, poverty, and violence from all around the globe. It is so easy to slip into despair. Our hearts and heads constantly cor-roborate this evidence with our own personal experience.

As Paul continues his lengthy prayer for the Colossians, he points them back to the deliverance that they have experienced in Christ. He prays that they would be full of thanks to God for qualifying them "to share in the inheritance of the saints in light" (Colossians 1:12).

When it comes to "the domain of darkness," the Scriptures do not mince words. We are not mere victims of the darkness—we helped bring the darkness about. In a different letter, Paul writes that we "were by nature children of wrath" (Ephesians 2:3). Praise

. . . GIVING THANKS TO THE FATHER, WHO HAS QUALIFIED YOU TO SHARE IN THE INHERITANCE OF THE SAINTS IN THE LIGHT. HE HAS DELIVERED US FROM THE DOMAIN OF DARKNESS AND TRANSFERRED US TO THE KINGDOM OF HIS BELOVED SON, IN WHOM WE HAVE REDEMPTION, THE FORGIVENESS OF SINS.

COLOSSIANS 1:12–14

God, that is not the end of our story. Paul continues, "But God, being rich in mercy, because of the great love with which he loved us, even when we were dead in our trespasses, made us alive together with Christ" (Ephesians 2:4–5).

While we actively disqualified ourselves from fellowship with God, Christ himself has qualified us for redemption. He perfectly obeyed yet paid for our disobedience. As Paul writes, "For our sake he made him to be sin who knew no sin, so that in him we might become the righteousness of God" (2 Corinthians 5:21). We have been "delivered from the domain of darkness" and transferred "to the kingdom of his beloved Son" (Colossians 1:13).

While we are saved in an instant, our growth in Christlikeness, a journey known as sanctification, is an ongoing process. The gospel continues to change and transform us daily. We are no longer children of the darkness! We belong to the light and are invited to walk in the light (1 John 1:5–7). We need to be reminded of this deliverance daily when shame seeks to pull us into hiding or the darkness of this world seeks to snuff out our light.

- How does Paul describe the gospel in these verses? What imagery does he use?

- What did the domain of darkness look like in your life?

- What changed in your life when you initially came to know Christ? What is still changing today?

IMMEASURABLE POWER AND SPACIOUS LOVE

IDENTIFY

○ Do you struggle to understand God's love for you?

○ Is it hard for you to believe that God's plans for your life are deeper and wider than you could ever dream?

● MY HUSBAND LOVES A GOOD HOUSE PROJECT, which means that we have tape measures scattered throughout our home for easy access at any time. He is constantly writing down and assessing square footage. I instead prefer to eyeball things and use my arm as a measuring stick.

In today's powerful prayer for God's people, we see Paul addressing length, depth, and width, but for a far more significant purpose than furniture or housing projects. Paul's prayer for the Ephesians reveals that the deepest longing of his heart is that they would know the immeasurable and inexhaustible love of God.

It may seem to go without saying, but everything in the life of the believer flows from our understanding of God's love for us. If we are not deeply and daily convinced of his love, we will run around trying to garner affection, security, and approval from our circumstances and interactions with others.

The apostle John understood this and thus wrote to the early

—THAT YOU, BEING ROOTED AND GROUNDED IN LOVE, MAY HAVE STRENGTH TO COMPREHEND WITH ALL THE SAINTS WHAT IS THE BREADTH AND LENGTH AND HEIGHT AND DEPTH, AND TO KNOW THE LOVE OF CHRIST THAT SURPASSES KNOWLEDGE, THAT YOU MAY BE FILLED WITH ALL THE FULLNESS OF GOD.

EPHESIANS 3:17B–19

churches, "In this is love, not that we have loved God but that he has loved us and sent his Son to be the propitiation for our sins" (1 John 4:10). Even though we might intellectually agree with the idea that God loves us, many of us struggle to believe and experience that love in our daily lives. When fears show up in our lives, they can only be expelled by coming to know and believe the love which God has for us (1 John 4:18).

Paul prays that the eternally abundant love of God that overflows from the Trinity would leak down into the cracks and crevices of our daily rounds. He wants us to parent as those deeply loved by God. He wants us to work as those deeply loved by God. He wants us to suffer as those deeply loved by God. He wants us to serve as those deeply loved by God.

As we come to walk in the spaciousness of God's love for us, our faith is bolstered and our fears and insecurities shrink. The more we know of the kind intentions of God's will toward us, the more we begin to trust him to do immeasurably more than we could ever ask or think (Ephesians 3:20–21).

- Where do you run to find security and affirmation when you forget the depths of God's love for you?

- When is the last time you experienced and remembered how much God loves you?

- What fears do you find in your heart presently? How might a reminder of God's love expel those fears?

TAKE +
SHARE

Prayer is not a waste of time; rather, it is one of the most significant things we can do to remain actively connected with God and aligned with his purposes in our lives. This week, look for extra pockets of time that you can devote to praying some of these powerful prayers we have been studying. Maybe it's during car line or the few minutes before bed that you spend scrolling on your phone. Maybe it's your time in the shower or in line at the grocery store. Write out a list of 3–5 people whom you want to pray for more consistently. Find a specific verse or verses to pray for each person (consider using Paul's prayers from Colossians 1:9–14 to get you started).

W ③

We all place something or someone at the center of our lives. Our security is in direct proportion to the strength and ability of whatever we place in the center. Only a life centered on Jesus Christ will be able to hold together! This week we will take a deeper look at Jesus, who alone is able to bring security to our lives.

CENTERED ON JESUS

THE CONTENT OF OUR PRAYERS

IDENTIFY

○ What are you tempted to make the center of your life?

○ What happens when that false center is shaken?

AT LEAST ONCE EVERY FEW MONTHS, I end up in a puddle of tears. Despite my best efforts to plan, keep the house stocked with food, juggle the children's sports schedules, and keep up with the members of our church, I end up dropping a ball. Either I miss an appointment or double-book appointments. I end up late to my son's basketball game or miss the birthday of a significant person in my life.

While I dread these moments when I can't keep all the plates spinning perfectly, I am learning to see them as little reminders from God that I am not the one at the center who holds everything together. He is.

When we place anything else at the center of our lives, even good things—like my desire to keep all my ducks in a row—we experience insecurity. Jobs, friendships, finances, the success of our kids—these are all amazing gifts, but they are unable to anchor our hearts. When we place the weight of our hopes on Jesus, we

HE IS THE IMAGE OF THE INVISIBLE GOD, THE FIRSTBORN OF ALL CREATION. FOR BY HIM, ALL THINGS WERE CREATED, IN HEAVEN AND ON EARTH, VISIBLE AND INVISIBLE, WHETHER THRONES OR DOMIN-IONS OF RULERS OR AUTHORITIES—ALL THINGS WERE CREAT-ED THROUGH HIM AND FOR HIM. AND HE IS BE-FORE ALL THINGS, AND IN HIM ALL THINGS HOLD TOGETHER.

COLOSSIANS 1:15-17

know that he can carry them as he carries us (Isaiah 46:3–4). Even the best gifts of this earth are subject to change and decay; however, we never have to worry that God's love, commitment, power, or plan will change (Hebrews 13:8).

In today's Scripture passage, we see that Paul desperately wants the Colossians to remember that they serve the God who holds everything together perfectly with his power. They, like us, were prone to forget that God is central. When we know that God holds everything together with perfect wisdom and sovereign power, we live our lives with greater peace and more appropriate purpose.

Paul reminds the Colossians that Christ is the invisible God made visible. The writer of the book of Hebrews says something very similar: "He is the radiance of the glory of God and the exact imprint of his nature, and he upholds the universe by the word of his power" (Hebrews 1:3).

No matter our circumstances, no matter our stresses or the demands on our time, as believers, we have eternal security knowing that Christ holds everything together and works everything for our good (Romans 8:28–32).

CONSIDER

- What words and images does Paul use to describe Christ in these verses? According to these verses, what did Christ create and what does he maintain?

- What happens when you put other things or people at the center?

- How does it change your life to know that Jesus is at the center of all things, holding all things together?

SECURITY FROM AUTHORITY

IDENTIFY

○ When you think of authority, what words, images, or phrases come to mind?

○ What benefits come from being under loving authority?

● OUR CULTURE and our flesh love the idea of freedom and cringe when we hear the word *authority*. Media constantly sells the prevailing worldview that authority kills our joy and freedom. We want freedom from all demands and expectations, yet we also want security and structure. The world is constantly promising and underdelivering.

Thankfully, God speaks to us according to truth and always delivers on his promises. The Christian worldview is honest about our human condition—it tells us that we are dignified yet dependent. We are incredibly significant, yet we are creatures under authority (Psalm 8:3–6).

A right understanding of God's good dominion leads us to more joy, freedom, and security, not less. Just as children can rest in the presence of their parents who provide both care and structure, we are invited to rest in the presence of God who is our loving authority.

AND HE IS THE HEAD OF THE BODY, THE CHURCH. HE IS THE BEGINNING, THE FIRSTBORN FROM THE DEAD, THAT IN EVERYTHING HE MIGHT BE PREEMINENT. FOR IN HIM ALL THE FULLNESS OF GOD WAS PLEASED TO DWELL, AND THROUGH HIM TO RECONCILE TO HIMSELF ALL THINGS, WHETHER ON EARTH OR IN HEAVEN, MAKING PEACE BY THE BLOOD OF HIS CROSS.

COLOSSIANS 1:18-20

Today, Paul continues his argument for the preeminence and supremacy of Christ by describing him as the head of the church (Colossians 1:18) and the very fullness of God himself (1:19). Contrary to popular belief, the head of the church is not the pastor or even the elders who are to help serve the church as servant leaders. Christ is the head of the church, and this gives us great hope. Christ is at the helm of his people and says with confidence, "I will build my church and the gates of hell shall not prevail against it" (Matthew 16:18). This provides incredible security for the believer in a terribly insecure world.

While we may think that taking a look at Jesus's power and supremacy might make us feel insecure (after all, a right view of him gives us a right view of our own dependence and inadequacies), understanding his power has the opposite effect. When we know that the God who saves us is sovereign and in control of all things, we can rest our lives (including our worries, our cares, our concerns, and our identities) securely upon him. This security comes from knowing he is good, gracious, faithful, and is lovingly committed to his people.

CONSIDER

- How does Paul describe Christ in these verses? What titles does he assign to him?

- How does Jesus's authority change the way we live?

- When is it hard for you to submit to the authority of Christ? Why do you think this is so?

RECONCILED TO GOD

IDENTIFY

○ How do you respond to conflict and tension?

○ Where in your life are you presently longing for peace?

I DON'T KNOW ABOUT YOU, but I detest even the mildest forms of tension or hostility. When my children argue or are at odds with one another, it breaks my heart and fills me with turmoil. Relational disharmony disturbs us because God created us for fourfold peace: peace with God, peace with others, peace within, and peace with the created world. Thus, even small breaches of trust or tension in our significant relationships remind us that we live in a broken world that needs restoration.

Lack of harmony and the presence of enmity bother us in human relationships, but they lead to death in our relationship with God. God felt the tearing tension of our broken relationship with him. He continually offered himself to his people who continually rejected him and his laws. He kept speaking even when his people would not listen. Rather than be at odds with us eternally, he chose to send Jesus, the second Person of the Trinity, to make peace through his cross. While we were still his enemies,

ALL THIS IS FROM GOD, WHO THROUGH CHRIST RECONCILED US TO HIMSELF AND GAVE US THE MINISTRY OF RECONCILIATION.

2 CORINTHIANS 5:18

Christ died for us, the just for the unjust that he might reconcile us to God (Romans 5:10; 1 Peter 3:18).

We don't use the word *reconcile* very much these days. After all, people used to reconcile their checkbooks with their actual bank accounts, but who uses checkbooks anymore? On occasion, we might hear the word used in a courtroom setting. Usually, reconciliation only comes up when we are speaking about two deeply opposed parties. This makes sense, as the Greek word for "reconciliation" (*katallassó*) means the moment when two opposed parties come to the same position.

Although we were created to exist in harmony with God as his beloved children, our sins threw up a massive wall of hostility between us (Isaiah 59:2). Because God did not want us to live in separation from him he sent his Son to bring us back to himself. This was a costly gift that came at the cost of Christ's very life.

As we walk with God, who has reconciled us to himself, we are invited into the ministry of reconciliation. We serve as ambassadors of Christ every time we display forgiveness or take steps toward restoration in our relationships. Moving closer to those who oppose us or have hurt us is countercultural and counterintuitive. But in light of what Jesus has done for us, Scripture encourages us to show one another honor and to do everything we can to live peaceably with one another (Romans 12:16–18).

When a friend slights us, we remember God's graciousness toward us. When our spouse's words hurt us, we remember God's healing words to us when we have hurt him. When a work conflict boils up, we seek to act as careful listeners to both sides. As those with whom God has made peace, we seek to spread peace.

WE SERVE AS AMBASSADORS OF CHRIST EVERY TIME WE DISPLAY FORGIVENESS OR TAKE STEPS TOWARD RESTORATION IN OUR RELATIONSHIPS.

CONSIDER

- How does Paul describe Christ's work of reconciliation?

- Where are you experiencing tension or disharmony in your relationship with God? In your relationships with others?

- How can you remember Christ's work of reconciliation? Where can you move toward others with the ministry of reconciliation?

CHRIST-CENTERED IDENTITY

IDENTIFY

○ When you describe yourself, what words do you most often use?

○ How do you think God sees you?

 EVERY TIME I drop my children off somewhere, I say the same thing before they close the door: "Act like a Joseph." While they sometimes roll their eyes at our little routine, they have come to expect the reminder to act like who they already are.

As children of the Joseph family household, there are certain principles by which we live; however, these principles don't make them a Joseph. Their actions are to flow from their identity. We daily remind them of who they are as they walk into a world screaming a thousand other potential identities at them. The apostle Paul does something similar in his letter to the Colossians.

He wants them to remember who they once were and who they now are. Though they were once "alienated and hostile in mind, doing evil deeds" (1:21), that is no longer their deepest identity or reality. Though they were once not a people, now they are God's people (Hosea 2:23).

By God's grace, all who call trust in Christ are welcomed into

AND YOU, WHO ONCE WERE ALIENATED AND HOSTILE IN MIND, DOING EVIL DEEDS, HE HAS NOW RECONCILED IN HIS BODY OF FLESH BY HIS DEATH, IN ORDER TO PRESENT YOU HOLY AND BLAMELESS AND ABOVE REPROACH BEFORE HIM.

COLOSSIANS 1:21–22

God's family not only as adopted sons and daughters but also as heirs of God's glorious inheritance (Romans 8:16–17). The deep identity spoken over the early church is true of us: "But you are a chosen race, a royal priesthood, a holy nation, a people for his own possession" (1 Peter 2:9a).

Praise God, through Christ, we are now holy and blameless. Or, as Paul continued in his letter to Titus, "But when the goodness and lovingkindness of God our Savior appeared, he saved us, not because of works done by us in righteousness, but according to his own mercy" (Titus 3:4–5). In Christ, we are declared holy and blameless. Now we get to live out of that deep declaration.

When shame tells us we are a failure, we remember that we are God's workmanship, his masterpiece (Ephesians 2:8–10). When the enemy counts off our sins, we see that as an opportunity to remember that she who has been much forgiven loves much (Luke 7:47). When we remember our secure identity in Christ, we are finally free from incessant worry about our standing. Instead of looking to others to tell us who we are (or remind us of who we aren't), we are able to lovingly tell them who God says they are.

CONSIDER

- What does it mean that we were alienated and hostile in mind? What did that look like in your life before Christ?

- Where are you currently struggling to believe that Christ declares you "holy and blameless"?

- What is one way to better align your actions with your deep identity in Christ?

FROM RESTLESS TO ROOTED

IDENTIFY

○ Where are you experiencing instability in your life right now?

○ What pressures tend to push you away from your hope in the gospel?

● OVER TWO HUNDRED YEARS AGO, French diplomat Alexis de Tocqueville came from Europe to learn about life in America. Among many other things, he noted a unique restlessness and rootlessness. He wrote, "At first sight there is something surprising in this strange unrest of so many happy men, restless amongst abundance. The spectacle itself, however, is as old as the world; the novelty is to see a whole people furnish an exemplification of it."[1] While he was surprised to see a whole nation of restless people, he also recognized that such instability was common to human experience.

The Scriptures tell a similar story of rootlessness and restlessness apart from God. Even though God constantly told his people he would protect them, they continually ran to Egypt and other nations for refuge (Isaiah 30:1–2). Even though today we are not literally running to Egypt, we do something similar when we look to other people or things to give us what only the Creator rightly can. We try a new church, move to a new house, and look for a better job. We expect an exotic vacation to give our souls rest when only God coming to Christ can do that (Matthew 11:28–30). Thankfully, the Bible invites us to a rooted stability that can be found only in a relationship with God. The gospel invites us to repent of our restlessness and to root our identities in the work and person of Christ!

In our verse today, Paul was writing to those who had already trusted in Christ for their salvation and secured themselves to the family of God and eternal hope. They had begun well, but Paul wanted them to finish well.

He did not want them to be *dislodged* (*metakineo*) from the firm foundation of Christ. Surrounded by the pull of short-lived, lesser hopes, he invites them to be anchored into the lasting hope of Christ. He longs for them to be firmly established (*themelius*), fixed, and well-stationed (*hedraios*) on the sure foundation of Christ.

We, like the Colossians, are also invited to stake our hopes for satisfaction and purpose on Jesus, who never changes. Rather than running to new material things. relationships, or circumstances, we have an opportunity to build a deepening relationship with the Lord— an unchanging foundation from which to weather the storms in life. Rather than building our lives on the shifting sands of circumstances, we are invited to build our lives securely on the unshakeable rock of Christ (Matthew 7:24–27).

...IF INDEED YOU CONTINUE IN THE FAITH, STABLE AND STEADFAST, NOT SHIFTING FROM THE HOPE OF THE GOSPEL THAT YOU HEARD, WHICH HAS BEEN PROCLAIMED IN ALL CREATION UNDER HEAVEN, AND OF WHICH I, PAUL, BECAME A MINISTER.

COLOSSIANS 1:23

Christ will keep those who continue to run to him as their refuge and cling to him in their need (1 Peter 1:3–5). Though the strength of their faith may wax and wane, the object of their faith remains strong and steadfast. The writer of the Hebrews says it this way, "Let us run with endurance the race that is set before us, looking to Jesus, the founder and perfecter of our faith" (Hebrews 12:1–2).

CONSIDER

- Where and when do you experience rest-lessness in your life?

- When are you most tempted to loosen your hands from clinging to hope in Christ? What lesser hopes are you tempted to grab instead?

- Read Philippians 1:6. What is God's part in helping us to hold fast?

TAKE + SHARE

Christ is the only fitting foundation for our lives. Every other person or pursuit we place at the center will crumble and fail. As you go about your week, ask your friends, neighbors, or coworkers about their biggest hopes and dreams. This can spark conversation about where they are placing their confidence. Pray for an open door to share where your confidence and hope come from.

W **4**

Walking and growing with Christ is the ongoing process of a lifetime. As we increase in spiritual maturity, we will experience more of the stability and security of a life centered upon him. The Scriptures do not tell us that life with Christ will be easy; however, God has given us all we need for fruitfully following him!

LIFE WITH CHRIST

SUFFERING WITH CHRIST

IDENTIFY

○ What is your immediate response to suffering?

○ Where do you run when life doesn't make sense?

I DON'T KNOW ABOUT YOU, but when suffering hits, I am usually shocked and surprised. Even though I have memorized Peter's admonition, "Beloved, do not be surprised at the fiery trial when it comes upon you to test you" (1 Peter 4:12), I always find myself surprised and punched in the gut when trials come. Pain and suffering literally take the breath out of us, yet suffering is a significant part of life with God on this side of glory.

Every worldview (way of making sense of the world) or religion must wrestle with the problem of pain and suffering; but only Christianity offers a Savior who experienced suffering willingly on our behalf. At the center of our faith stands One with outstretched, wounded hands welcoming us into his presence and willing to be with us in our pain.

In today's verse, Paul talks about filling up what is lacking in the afflictions of Christ. This does not mean that Christ's suffering was not sufficient for our sin; rather, it means that when we

NOW I REJOICE IN MY SUFFERINGS FOR YOUR SAKE, AND IN MY FLESH I AM FILLING UP WHAT IS LACKING IN CHRIST'S AFFLICTIONS FOR THE SAKE OF THE BODY, THAT IS, THE CHURCH.

COLOSSIANS 1:24

suffer for righteousness, we have a chance to live out Jesus's willing-to-suffer love. Paul saw suffering as an opportunity to show off the sufficiency of his Savior. In his experiences of suffering, he sought to draw near to the One who suffered to the point of death on the cross (Hebrews 12:1–4).

The life, death, and resurrection of Christ inform and transform our suffering on this earth. For the believer, suffering comes with two guarantees: it does not last forever, and it is purposeful. God will make beauty from our ashes (Isaiah 61:1–3; 1 Peter 1:6–9). In our suffering, we have an opportunity to point to the Suffering Savior and to share in his

likeness (1 Peter 4:12–14). We never suffer alone, but rather, we are comforted by the indwelling Spirit who helps us in our weakness (Romans 8:26–27). God also uses our experience of suffering to produce growth in endurance, character, and hope in us (Romans 5:3–5).

When suffering knocks the breath out of our lungs, we remember him who breathed his last breath on a painful cross. We also remember that Christ does not move away from our messes and our pain—he steps toward us and meets us in them. As we learn to do life with God, we begin to know the God who is with us in our suffering.

CONSIDER

- What suffering are you or your loved ones experiencing in this season? What is your response to that suffering?

- How does the reality of Christ's suffering change the way we think of and experience suffering on the earth?

- Describe a time when you were able to say with Paul, "I rejoice in my sufferings" because of Christ's presence and purpose.

AN INVITATION TO INTIMACY WITH GOD

IDENTIFY

○ What is the most significant invitation you have ever received?

○ How do you respond to God's invitation to intimacy with him?

● REMEMBER THE STORY of Zacchaeus? When it is taught in Sunday school classes, we focus so much on his short stature and his penchant for climbing trees. But the story is really about the incredible invitation of Christ to a most unlikely follower. I bet Zacchaeus nearly fell out of that sycamore tree when he realized that not only did Jesus know him, but he also wanted to visit his home (Luke 19:1–10).

No wonder he hightailed it down from that tree branch. Jesus wanted to be with him—the corrupt tax collector whom everyone else despised! As shocking as this might have been for Zacchaeus, the invitation held out to us as believers in Christ is even more astonishing: God will dwell within us, or as Paul describes it, "Christ in you, the hope of glory" (Colossians 1:27).

The prophet Isaiah only partially understood the glories he predicted and prophesied when God said, "I dwell in the high and holy place, and also with him who is of a contrite and lowly spirit,

...OF WHICH I BECAME A MINISTER ACCORDING TO THE STEWARDSHIP FROM GOD THAT WAS GIVEN TO ME FOR YOU, TO MAKE THE WORD OF GOD FULLY KNOWN, THE MYSTERY HIDDEN FOR AGES AND GENERATIONS BUT NOW REVEALED TO HIS SAINTS. TO THEM GOD CHOSE TO MAKE KNOWN HOW GREAT AMONG THE GENTILES ARE THE RICHES OF THE GLORY OF THIS MYSTERY, WHICH IS CHRIST IN YOU, THE HOPE OF GLORY.

COLOSSIANS 1:25–27

to revive the spirit of the lowly, and to revive the heart of the contrite" (Isaiah 57:15).

The holy God of the universe always intended to make his home in the hearts of his people (John 14:23). This is the transcendent (far off; other than) God made imminent (incredibly near and close to). The presence of God used to dwell in one specific place for a season (first the tabernacle and then the Holy of Holies in the temple); however, through the indwelling Holy Spirit, our very bodies become the permanent residing place of the Spirit of God (2 Chronicles 7:1–16; 1 Corinthians 6:19).

A significant part of following Jesus is realizing that God wants to do life with us. In fact, through the indwelling Spirit, God lives within us! The sheer audacity of this invitation should shock us the way Jesus's invitation shocked Zacchaeus. Who are we to receive such an unthinkable invitation and to experience such intimacy with God?

When we begin to understand that God wants to do life with us, it changes the way we see the normal events of our lives. Small things that seem insignificant are now infused with meaning and company. Christ is with us; thus, we have great hope!

CONSIDER

- Read John 14:15–24. What do you learn about the indwelling Spirit from these words of Jesus?

- How would it change the way you lived if you constantly remembered that your body is a temple in which God dwells?

- Describe a time when you experienced the nearness of God in the middle of the mundane.

RELEARNING TO ABIDE

IDENTIFY

○ Do you struggle to experience God during the realities of daily life?

○ Do you long for his presence as you are about your normal routine?

● DO YOU EVER FEEL a massive gap between your Sundays and your Mondays? Between your moments with the Lord and the remaining moments of your day? As we learn to do life with God, we soon realize that there is often dissonance between the truths our minds know and our lived experience of those truths. Only as we learn to abide in Christ will the gaps between our Sundays and Mondays and our heads and hearts shrink.

One of the word pictures God gives us in the Old Testament is that of his people being a vine he planted with great care (Isaiah 5:1–2). Isaiah paints the word picture of a master gardener doing everything in his power to set up his vine for success. Likewise, when God created Adam and Eve, he gave them everything they needed to thrive, most notably full access to himself. Unfortunately, because of mankind's rebellion against our good God, the vine went wild, continually bent on going astray from God's good purposes (Isaiah 5:3–7).

ABIDE IN ME, AND I IN YOU. AS THE BRANCH CANNOT BEAR FRUIT BY ITSELF, UNLESS IT ABIDES IN THE VINE, NEITHER CAN YOU, UNLESS YOU ABIDE IN ME. I AM THE VINE; YOU ARE THE BRANCHES. WHOEVER ABIDES IN ME AND I IN HIM, HE IT IS THAT BEARS MUCH FRUIT, FOR APART FROM ME YOU CAN DO NOTHING:

JOHN 15:4–5

When Jesus was on the earth, he identified himself as "the true vine" and his father as "the vinedresser" (John 15:1). In some of his final words to his disciples, Jesus commanded them to abide in him like branches abide in the vine. He holds the same invitation out to us today.

When we abide in Christ, we cling to him, depend on him, and trust him for our all we need. This could mean intentionally handing him our anxieties, asking for wisdom for handling a difficult situation, or asking him to keep our eyes open for how he wants us to bless others as we go about each day. As a branch cannot exist without the sap provided by the vine, we admit that are entirely dependent upon God's grace to give us all we need for life and godliness (2 Peter 1:3).

When we actively abide in Jesus, we trust him to hold us up and support us throughout all the seasons of our lives. We admit our inability to bear fruit apart from his grace. We rest the weight of our fears and hopes on him alone (Philippians 4:4–6).

As we walk with our Lord in this way, we begin to experience his nearness not only on Sundays but throughout our entire week.

AS WE LEARN TO DO LIFE

WITH GOD, WE SOON

REALIZE THAT THERE IS

OFTEN DISSONANCE

BETWEEN THE TRUTHS

OUR MINDS KNOW AND OUR

LIVED EXPERIENCE OF

THOSE TRUTHS.

CONSIDER

- What does the vine offer to the branch? How does a branch abide in the vine?

- Describe a time when you experienced abiding in Christ. What did it look like?

- What daily rhythms and routines can help you to abide in Christ?

MOVING TOWARD MATURITY

IDENTIFY

○ What benchmarks signal spiritual maturity?

○ How do you know if you are becoming more mature in your relationship with God?

OUR FAMILY LOVES AVOCADOS in all their forms, most notably guacamole and avocado toast. Seeing as we live in southern California with a climate conducive to avocado trees, I thought we would give growing them a try. The price difference between a mature avocado plant and a juvenile plant shocked me, so I went with the young avocado plant. Big mistake.

Apparently, there is a reason mature avocado plants cost so much: it takes younger trees three to four years to bear fruit and *up to thirteen years* if you start with a seed!

Growing toward maturity is always a process, whether you are a plant or a person. If it takes years for an avocado plant to mature, how much more a human soul! While most of us want to be mature, we often struggle to appreciate or leave space for the long, slow processes involved in developing from spiritual infancy to maturity.

In today's passage, the apostle Paul clearly tells the Colossians

HIM WE PROCLAIM, WARNING EVERY-ONE AND TEACHING EVERYONE WITH ALL WISDOM, THAT WE MAY PRESENT EVERYONE MATURE IN CHRIST.

COLOSSIANS 1:28

that the goal of his ministry is present believers "mature in Christ." In the next chapter, Paul offers more details about what he means when he speaks of this growth. Those who are mature in Christ continue to walk with him, grow deep roots in him, and build wisely upon the sturdy foundation of Christ (Colossians 2:6–7). They hold tightly to the truths they receive and approach life with a spirit of gratitude and thankfulness (v. 7).

Underlying these verses is the reality that growing toward maturity is a process that takes intentionality and effort. Like any organic process, growth is often slow and imperceptible. Personal change comes through a series of small, faithful, daily choices, and it is easy to grow weary and to lose heart along the way. Paul reminds us that we will indeed reap what we sow, however. If we sow to please the Spirit, we will reap a harvest of spiritual maturity in due time (Galatians 6:7–9).

Life with God involves the slow process of growing toward maturity, yet we know that, by God's grace, we will be transformed "from one degree of glory to another" (2 Corinthians 3:18). That's a beautiful harvest worth pursuing!

CONSIDER

- Read Ephesians 4:11–16. What do these verses say about the role of community in growth toward maturity in Christ?

- Where do you see hints of spiritual immaturity remaining in your own heart and life presently?

- Where do you see evidence of God slowly but surely moving you toward more maturity in him?

STRAINING TOWARD CHRIST

IDENTIFY

○ What accomplishment are you most proud of?

○ What kind of effort and work did you exert toward this goal?

○ Were you ever tempted to quit?

● IN COLLEGE, my Bible study leader convinced me it would be a great idea to run a marathon with her. We found the simplest training plan and bought all the required running gear. It turns out that *simple*, however, is not the same as *easy*.

In the Christian life, sometimes we tend to confuse effort with earning and simple with easy. Grace means that we have unearned favor with God; but, living out of grace requires great effort—we must constantly choose to live out of the strength and grace God gives us and remain active participants in his transformative work in our lives. Life with God is simple (straightforward), but that does not mean living the Christian life comes naturally.

As believers, we have done nothing to merit or earn our standing before God. We stand approved before God only based on the completed work of Jesus on our behalf. However, when it comes to growing in Christ, we sometimes begin to think that it will be

FOR THIS I TOIL, STRUGGLING WITH ALL HIS ENERGY THAT HE POWERFULLY WORKS WITHIN ME.

COLOSSIANS 1:29

an effortless or easy process.

In our verse today, Paul is not afraid to use words like "toil" and "struggle" when he speaks about his ministry. In fact, the Greek word *agonizomai* translated "struggle" is the root word for the modern English word "agonize." Initially, this might begin to sound like bad news rather than good news. However, God not only commands our obedience but also empowers us for obedience. Yes, there is strain, but there is also his strength.

God offers us access to his unlimited, inexhaustible strength and power. Part of union with Christ is unhindered access to his storehouses of strength. In his letter to the Philippians, Paul writes, "Work out your own salvation with fear and trembling, for it is God who works in you, both to will and to work for his good pleasure" (Philippians 2:12–13).

We are to work hard with fear and trembling; yet God is working in us. We are working out what Christ has worked in us. As we do life with God, we labor with the strength that our Savior provides. God promises that all who trust him will reach the finish line. He also promises to be with us all along the way.

- Reread Colossians 1:10–11. Where do you see our effort and God's strength in these verses?

- Where are you experiencing toil and struggle in your walk with God presently?

- What practices help you to rely more fully on God's strength rather than your own?

TAKE +
SHARE

The more we experience the security of life with God, even with its suffering and strain, the more we long for others to experience life with God. Write down the names of two to three people who you want to see grow in spiritual maturity. Pray for them daily this week, asking God for ways to come alongside him in presenting them mature in Christ. Consider writing a note of encouragement to one or all of them.

W ⑤

We often read the Scriptures through an individualistic lens; however, God intends us to live the Christian life within a vibrant community of faith. Apart from community, we will not experience the full security offered to us in Christ. This week, we will explore the role of community in moving us toward spiritual maturity.

STANDING FIRM IN THE FAITH

FIRM
FAITH

IDENTIFY

○ What words would you use to describe the current condition of your faith?

○ Who helps you stand firm in your faith? How?

● SOMETIMES MY FAITH feels solid and firm, but at other times, my faith feels wobbly and weak. I long to walk steadily with confident faith, but I often find my feet starting to slip and totter by doubt, distraction, or fear. I am thankful for God's Word, especially the psalms that remind me that my experience is not uncommon. The writers of the psalms admitted many times that it felt like their faith was wavering, yet God held them fast (Psalms 73:2, 23–24; 94:18–19; 121:3–4).

In today's verses, we get a glimpse into Paul's prayers for the Colossians whom he had never even met. Paul tells them that he struggled in prayer that their faith might be firm and their confidence in Christ complete (Colossians 2:1–2). Apparently, Paul took prayer very seriously. The word *agon* translated *struggle*, in the first verse of this chapter, literally referred to the athletic contests people were accustomed to in the ancient Isthmian games.

Paul wrestled and agonized as he prayed for these young churches, but he wasn't praying to secure their material prosperity.

FOR I WANT YOU TO KNOW HOW GREAT A STRUGGLE I HAVE FOR YOU AND FOR THOSE AT LAODICEA AND FOR ALL WHO HAVE NOT SEEN ME FACE TO FACE, THAT THEIR HEARTS MAY BE ENCOURAGED, BEING KNIT TOGETHER IN LOVE, TO REACH ALL THE RICHES OF FULL ASSURANCE OF UNDERSTANDING AND THE KNOWLEDGE OF GOD'S MYSTERY, WHICH IS CHRIST, IN WHOM ARE HIDDEN ALL THE TREASURES OF WISDOM AND KNOWLEDGE.

COLOSSIANS 2:1-3

He did not ask for property for a church building. He begged God that their hearts would be knit together in love. He did not pray that their pockets would be filled. Rather, he prayed that together as a community they would know the fullness available to them in the person of Christ. He did not pray for them to have storehouses of success and comfort. Rather, he prayed that they would have eyes to see the storehouses of understanding and knowledge hidden in the person of Christ (v. 2).

The imagery Paul uses as he prays for the unity of the believers in Colossae offers a powerful picture of the communal nature of the Christian life. Christ's love knits us together with those who are different from us and gives us new eyes to see one another as brothers and sisters in Christ (1 Corinthians 12:12–13). Christ's love connects us to a community of others who are growing and being transformed into his likeness. When we are struggling or need courage, the body of Christ can hold us up and remind us of what is true.

With Christ, we can stand firm even when all the circumstances around us feel unstable and insecure. We have him, and having him, we have everything we need. When our faith begins to falter and we begin to forget the faithfulness of God, our community helps to steady us as they remind us, through their lives and their words: Jesus will hold us fast!

CONSIDER

● Describe a season when
  God upheld you despite
  your wavering faith.
  What helped to make
  your faith firmer?

● According to these
  verses, what role does
  community play in
  growing toward confi-
  dence in Christ?

● Is there someone in your
  faith community God
  might be calling you to
  encourage? How might
  you seek to strengthen
  their faith this week?

THE DANGER OF COUNTERFEIT TRUTHS

IDENTIFY

○ What lies try to weaken your faith?

○ What helps you stand firm in your faith?

● PROFESSIONAL COUNTERFEITERS would never try to pay for clothes or groceries with Monopoly money. When seeking to deceive shopkeepers and checkout clerks, they must make fake money that looks deceivingly like the real thing. The same is true with false teachers and the enemy of God. When attempting to deceive and delude believers, they make use of fine-sounding, "plausible arguments" (v. 4).

Concern over false teachings (heresies) was the impetus of Paul's letter to the Colossians. Through various messengers in his band of brothers, Paul had received word that the church planted in Colossae was beginning to succumb to various threads of lies or half-truths from the surrounding cultures. Counterfeit gospels were leaking into their hearts and minds.

Paul is concerned that these believers will be deluded by fine-sounding arguments, and he wants these believers to be aware that they are surrounded by spiritual powers, principalities,

I SAY THIS IN ORDER THAT NO ONE MAY DELUDE YOU WITH PLAUSIBLE ARGUMENTS. FOR THOUGH I AM ABSENT IN BODY, YET I AM WITH YOU IN SPIRIT, REJOICING TO SEE YOUR GOOD ORDER AND THE FIRMNESS OF YOUR FAITH IN CHRIST.

COLOSSIANS 2:4-5

and conniving people intending to pull them away from the rock-solid foundation of the gospel (Ephesians 6:12). The lies to which we most easily succumb are not outright, ridiculous falsehoods but rather shades and distortions of things that are partial truths. As such, Paul struggles in prayer on their behalf, knowing that "the weapons of our warfare are not of the flesh but have divine power to destroy strongholds" (2 Corinthians 10:4).

Though our circumstances may look vastly different from the church at Colossae, we share a similar susceptibility to false "truths." The culture tells us, "Be true to yourself" and, "All paths lead to God." Both ideas trigger pleasant feelings about following our hearts and going with what "feels right" over a worldview shaped by the truths of God's Word.

As we continue to fix our eyes on Christ, we will become more aware of counterfeits. As we cling to God's Word, we will stand firm in our faith, unmoved by persuasive arguments that would lead us away from the truth of the gospel.

CONSIDER

- What are some of the plausible and fine-sounding false arguments that might delude the church today?

- What half-truths or lies shake you personally from firmness of faith?

- What truths about Christ do you need to remember to help anchor your faith?

METAPHORS FOR MATURITY

IDENTIFY

○ When you think of a mature believer,
what images come to mind?

● IF THE APOSTLE PAUL were to sit in a high school
English class, his teacher would probably roll his or her eyes at his
penchant for mixed metaphors. It is not uncommon for his letters
to begin with one analogy or metaphor and then suddenly switch
to another. Paul, like many of the authors inspired by the Spirit to
write the Scriptures, sought to capture eternal, unseen realities
through the limitations of human words and experiences.

In today's verses, Paul offers multiple word pictures describing
maturity in Christ: a journey, a tree, and a building upon a foundation. Paul also likens deepening faith in Christ to a race or a
journey (Acts 20:24; 2 Timothy 4:7). He reminds the Colossians that
they must continue to put one foot in front of the other to follow
Christ and not fall away into false teachings (Colossians 2:6).

Next, Paul encourages them to grow their roots deeply in the
soil of God's love (v. 7). The Scriptures continually paint the picture of the mature man or woman of God as a tree with deep
roots and flourishing shoots (Psalm 1; Jeremiah 17:7–8). Trees

BELIEVE

THEREFORE, AS YOU RECEIVED CHRIST JESUS THE LORD, SO WALK IN HIM, ROOTED AND BUILT UP IN HIM AND ESTABLISHED IN THE FAITH, JUST AS YOU WERE TAUGHT, ABOUNDING IN THANKSGIVING.

COLOSSIANS 2:6–7

with resilient roots reach deep to find sustenance and strength and are secure even in drought.

Why did Paul spend so much time drawing elaborate pictures of mature faith? What's at stake if we remain immature? According to the apostle James, quite a bit! If we settle for an immature faith and waiver in doubt, we will be easily moved and tossed about by every wind of trouble that hits us (James 1:6). According to Jesus in his parable of the sower, if we do not move toward maturity, we risk the shoots of our faith being easily scorched by the sun and withering away (Matthew 21:5–8).

Our broken world is a far cry from a gentle greenhouse. When suffering comes into our lives, it will shake a shallow-rooted faith. When persecution or opposition push back on our beliefs, we need to be firmly planted in the deep soil of God's Word. Maturity matters because, as Jesus promised, "In the world you will have tribulation," (John 16:33).

When a loved one is hospitalized, we need a strong foundation of faith. When our dreams are met with disappointment, we need a firm faith in our faithful, sovereign God. When the world rejects us, we need to intimately know the Savior who says, "Take heart; I have overcome the world" (v. 33).

The closer we walk with Jesus, the deeper the roots of our faith will grow and the firmer our foundation will be.

IF WE SETTLE FOR AN IMMATURE FAITH AND WAIVER IN DOUBT, WE WILL BE EASILY MOVED AND TOSSED ABOUT BY EVERY WIND OF TROUBLE THAT HITS US.

CONSIDER

● Which of Paul's three analogies in these verses most resonate with you in this season? Why?

▬

● What trials or temptations are you presently experiencing? What are they teaching you about your faith?

▬

● Read Psalm 1. Pray for God to deepen your roots in him.

▬

CHRIST IS ENOUGH

IDENTIFY

○ Do you ever feel inadequate or like you don't have what you need?

○ In those moments, where do you run to find adequacy and security?

AT MY CATHOLIC SCHOOL growing up, we spent most of middle school memorizing all kinds of lists: personal pronouns, French verb conjugations, and every preposition in the English language. To this day, I can still sing the preposition jingle. I didn't realize then how much meaning could be held by such small, seemingly insignificant words. It seems that the apostle Paul understood the power of one simple prepositional phrase: *in him*.

The entire theological reality of union with Christ can be summed with the simple phrase "in him." These two little words, only five letters in total, carry life-changing freight. In union with Christ, everything changes for the believer.

The message of Christianity is not merely an invitation to imitate Christ, but also an invitation to participate in the very life of Christ. His perfect life becomes our life. His death becomes our death. His resurrection allows us to live in resurrection life. Paul offers a summary statement of these concepts when writing to

FOR IN HIM THE WHOLE FULLNESS OF DEITY DWELLS BODILY, AND YOU HAVE BEEN FILLED IN HIM, WHO IS THE HEAD OF ALL RULE AND AUTHORITY.

COLOSSIANS 2:9-10

the Galatians: "I have been crucified with Christ. It is no longer I who live, but Christ who lives in me" (Galatians 2:20).

In today's focal passage, Paul begins to address one of the false systems that was creeping into the Colossian church: ceremonialism. Paul's statement about circumcision might seem distant and confusing, but most of us can relate to conforming to culturally approved behaviors to feel confident and to gain a sense of belonging. We try to find security in knowing that we have fulfilled our obligations and met the expectations of others, but the only sure source of security is Christ.

Paul assures the saints at Colossae that the gospel works from the inside out, not the outside in. We don't become clean from outward acts of washing; we are clean because of the work of Christ (Matthew 23:26; John 15:3). Our security does not come from our ability to check all the right boxes; it comes from the One who lived a perfect life only to die an unjust death. Our confidence is not in our own performance but in the person of Christ. We don't need the world's latest self-help book when we realize that all the wisdom we need comes from God.

The key to learning to live a secure life in an insecure world is understanding all that we have access to in our union with Christ.

CONSIDER

- What are some examples of empty philosophies that fight to take our hearts and minds captive today?

- How would your life look different if you believed that you were filled with all fullness in Christ?

- Where are you wrongly deriving security from your own performance rather than the perfect work of Christ?

CHRIST BEARS OUR SHAME

IDENTIFY

○ What lies does shame whisper to you?

○ Who continues to faithfully remind you of your security in Christ?

IN 2010 researcher Brené Brown nearly broke the internet with her Ted Talk on shame. She gave word to the widespread feelings of shame that every person feels at some point. Brown described guilt as feelings of having done something bad, as compared to shaming which says, "I am bad." Shame is a buzzword in our culture today; however, the reality of shame is nearly as old as humanity.

Scripture addresses and explains both our guilt and our shame. Directly after transgressing the one command God gave them in the garden, we find a guilty Adam and Eve hiding in shame (Genesis 3:1–13). Once they walked away from their unbroken fellowship with their Creator, they instantly felt their unworthiness to stand before him. They knew something about them was wrong and broken. That feeling has never left mankind.

Paul explores the concept of shame in these verses to the Colossians. He knows these believers will continue to bump up against their failure to perform, but he has a liberating message to share with them: they don't have to live in shame anymore.

AND YOU, WHO WERE DEAD IN YOUR TRESPASSES, AND THE UNCIRCUMCISION OF YOUR FLESH, GOD MADE ALIVE TOGETHER WITH HIM, HAVING FORGIVEN US ALL OUR TRESPASSES BY CANCELING THE RECORD OF DEBT THAT STOOD AGAINST US WITH ITS LEGAL DEMANDS. THIS HE SET ASIDE, NAILING IT TO THE CROSS. HE DISARMED THE RULERS AND AUTHORITIES AND PUT THEM TO OPEN SHAME, BY TRIUMPHING OVER THEM IN HIM.

COLOSSIANS 2:13–15

Jesus set them free from their bondage to sin and their feelings of condemnation.

The presence of sin breeds feelings of unworthiness and insecurity, but Christ's blood speaks a better word over believers. We are the beloved children of God, those who were bought at a great price even while we were yet sinners (Romans 5:6–11; 1 Peter 1:18–19). Our transgressions have been paid for by Jesus on the cross. As a result of his finished work, it is now the enemies of God who are put to open shame, not the adopted children of the Lord.

Shame makes us want to hide and isolate ourselves. It says, "It they knew what you were really like, they would not love you." It reminds us of our failures and leaves us feeling help-less and worthless.

When shame hisses its loud lies at us, we who are in Christ can respond confidently that "the record of debt that stood against us" has been dealt with at the cross (Colossians 2:14). When shame wants us to hide in feelings of unworthiness, we remem-ber that we are children of the light, bought at the infinite price of the blood of Jesus. We say with confidence alongside the apostle John, "See what kind of love the Father has given to us, that we should be called children of God; and so we are" (1 John 3:1). We can now stand assured that we are accepted, for-given, made new, in the light, walking in our new nature as redeemed children of God.

CONSIDER

- When do you experience shame most often?

- Paul talks about the record of debt that stood against us. What are some of the things that the Enemy brings up from your own record of debt, sin, and shame?

- What practically helps you to remember that Christ has dealt with your sin and shame? What leads you to celebrate the triumph we have in Christ?

TAKE +
SHARE

It is challenging to stand firm in our faith in a world full of lies and with souls full of shame. Only when God's Word is the loudest voice in our lives will we be able to experience true security and confidence.

This is one reason we need other Christians speaking into our lives and helping us stand firm in our faith. This week, look for ways to creatively speak God's glorious promises over your family and friends, reminding them of who they are in Christ, how near and trustworthy he is, and how they can truly find rest in him. Write a note of encouragement, text a specific verse you are praying for them, or invite them out to coffee.

Our culture is constantly telling us that we don't have enough and that we need more—more clothes, updated phones, nicer cars, better furniture, and so on. While this may be a great strategy for marketing products, this sense of inadequacy could not be further from the truth! In Christ, we truly have all we need. He offers us wisdom, security, and peace that is found nowhere else! This week we will remember the sufficiency of Christ!

OUR ALL-SUFFICIENT SAVIOR

QUALIFIED BY CHRIST

IDENTIFY

○ What happens when you build your confidence on your performance or on the approval of others?

○ When was the last time you felt insufficient?

● DO YOU REMEMBER trying to write your first résumé? I recall spending hours in the computer lab trying to make myself stand out, highlighting what was special about my experience and abilities. While this may work for pursuing a job, it is a fatal approach to building spiritual confidence. We are conditioned to list off our accomplishments, knowledge, or spiritual pedigree to feel like we have "arrived." The reality, however, is that the résumé of every believer should simply say one thing: I trust in Christ alone.

Though the Colossians initially believed God's approval of them was based on the finished work of Christ, eventually they began to add to their proverbial résumés. They caved to the outward pressure of new religious teaching and began keeping a checklist of rituals and ceremonies for their sense of righteousness before God.

Rather than trust that Christ made them clean, they began

THEREFORE LET NO ONE PASS JUDGMENT ON YOU IN QUESTIONS OF FOOD AND DRINK, OR WITH REGARD TO A FESTIVAL OR A NEW MOON OR A SABBATH. THESE ARE A SHADOW OF THE THINGS TO COME, BUT THE SUBSTANCE BELONGS TO CHRIST.

COLOSSIANS 2:16-17

to think that washing rituals made them clean. They began to tether their confidence to their ability to keep man-made rules about how to dress, what to eat, or how to pray. Rather than being secure in who Jesus declared them to be, they began to give in to the scrutiny of others around them—the judgments of others who were living by a self-imposed checklist rather than resting in the finished work of Christ on their behalf.

We all know what it feels like to feel the weight of living up to expectations—whether others' or our own. We may begin to think that God loves us because of our regular church attendance. We may attach our security to a certain denomination or system of theology. While it's great to have a solid commitment to service, doctrine, and regular involvement in corporate worship, these activities are a poor source of security and righteousness.

The gospel invites us to stand firmly on the finished work of Christ. Nothing can shake our standing with him. When we are tempted to wonder what God thinks of us or whether we've done enough to make him happy, we must remember where our confidence comes from: "Such is the confidence that we have through Christ toward God. Not that we are sufficient in ourselves to claim anything as coming from us, but our sufficiency is from God" (2 Corinthians 3:4–5). There's nothing left to prove!

● From what external
behaviors (dos and
don'ts) do you draw
confidence and security?

▬▬▬

● What are some of the
lies that speak
judgment over you?

▬▬▬

● Reread 2 Corinthians
3:4–5. How does it
feel to remember
that your sufficiency
comes from God?

▬▬▬

SELF-MADE RELIGION AND THE GOD-GIVEN GOSPEL

IDENTIFY

○ What areas of your life are you currently seeking to improve?

○ How are you going about these attempts at self-mastery?

WHEN I HEAR the word *self-made*, I think of Benjamin Franklin. Rising from poverty and a lack of education to become an inventor, artist, and statesman. He literally became the typecast for the idealized American man. In college, I read his own account of his lofty attempt at moral perfection. Having identified thirteen core virtues, he would focus on one every week, scoring himself on his ability to live out each virtue with an actual scorecard. Franklin admitted how much he struggled to gain mastery, as he would improve in one virtue but slip into old patterns in the others.

His attempt made an impression on me, but not the way Franklin intended. Franklin's attempt at self-made mastery over his sinful nature only underscored to me our desperate need for the God-given gospel—that to-do list was exhausting and impossible! In today's verses, the apostle Paul attempts to say something similar to the young believers at Colossae.

IF WITH CHRIST YOU DIED TO THE ELEMENTAL SPIRITS OF THE WORLD, WHY, AS IF YOU WERE STILL ALIVE IN THE WORLD, DO YOU SUBMIT TO REGULATIONS—"DO NOT HANDLE, DO NOT TASTE, DO NOT TOUCH" (REFERRING TO THINGS THAT ALL PERISH AS THEY ARE USED)—ACCORDING TO HUMAN PRECEPTS AND TEACHINGS? THESE HAVE INDEED AN APPEARANCE OF WISDOM IN PROMOTING SELF-MADE RELIGION AND ASCETICISM AND SEVERITY TO THE BODY, BUT THEY ARE OF NO VALUE IN STOPPING THE INDULGENCE OF THE FLESH.

COLOSSIANS 2:20–23

The Colossians were being enticed by false teachers to practice severity to the body and to adhere to all kinds of outward rules and regulations that were not given by Christ. These systems, like Franklin's attempt at moral perfection, seemed to have the appearance of wisdom; however, Paul sternly reminds them that they are powerless to change the sin nature.

The love of God as shown through the life, death, and resurrection of Christ does what the law could never do. As God had promised his people long before the birth of Christ, "I will give you a new heart, and a new spirit I will put within you. . . . And I will put my Spirit within you, and cause you to walk in my statutes" (Ezekiel 36:26–27). Christ did not come to make bad people good. He came to make dead people alive in him. The God-given gospel does what man-made religion could never do.

CONSIDER

● What are some
present-day examples
of things that have the
appearance of wisdom
but are of no value in
stopping the flesh?

● Read James 3:17–18.
What do these verses
say about godly wisdom
(as compared to things
with the appearance of
wisdom)?

● Where have you seen
the gospel transform
you from the inside out?

ALWAYS IN NEED OF THE GOSPEL

IDENTIFY

○ How has your appreciation for the gospel changed since you first came to know Christ?

○ How often do you remember your need for grace?

● EVERY YEAR when summer is about to end and school is about to begin, I experience a mini moment of crisis. In summertime, my three sons live in bathing suits and athletic shorts. We give little thought to wardrobe during those glorious months of outdoor fun. But as school approaches, we must reassess the clothing situation in their closets. All their pants are now capris; their long-sleeved shirts are awkward three-quarter length. And don't even get me started on their shoes.

While we grow out of clothes, we never grow out of our need for the gospel. Sometimes we erroneously think of the gospel like college loans: we are given a gift on the front end that we slowly pay back with time, becoming less and less indebted to the one who gave the loan. This could not be further from the truth!

As we mature in our walks with God and seek to obey him, we only grow in our dependence upon God and indebtedness to his grace. The more we grow in godliness, the more we realize our

LET ME ASK YOU ONLY THIS: DID YOU RECEIVE THE SPIRIT BY WORKS OF THE LAW OR BY HEARING WITH FAITH? ARE YOU SO FOOLISH? HAVING BEGUN BY THE SPIRIT, ARE YOU NOW BEING PERFECTED BY THE FLESH?

GALATIANS 3:2-3

need for the gospel. At the beginning of his ministry, the apostle Paul referred to himself as the least of the apostles (1 Corinthians 15:9). Then in the middle of his ministry career, Paul called himself the least of the saints (Ephesians 3:8). At the end of his life, Paul identified himself as the chief of sinners (1 Timothy 1:15). It is not that Paul became more sinful as he matured spiritually; instead, he became more aware of his innate sinfulness and more dependent upon God's daily grace.

The simple steps that we took when we initially believed (repent and believe) are the same two steps that we keep taking every day as we walk with God. The dependence upon Jesus that initiated our walks with God will be the truth that leads us all the way into glory. We continue to repent and believe daily—not to secure our salvation, but to live rightly in reality. We admit our sin and our need for God's grace daily. We receive his forgiveness daily. We rely on his strength daily. As we do so, we glorify the One who is both the founder and finisher (perfecter) of our faith (Hebrews 12:2).

AS WE MATURE IN OUR WALKS WITH GOD AND SEEK TO OBEY HIM, WE ONLY GROW IN OUR DEPENDENCE UPON GOD AND INDEBTEDNESS TO HIS GRACE.

CONSIDER

- What is the Spirit's role in our ongoing sanctification (being made more like Jesus) as believers?

- Where are you relying on your own strength rather than the gospel to grow in godliness?

- What do you need to practically repent of today? What gospel truths do you need to believe today?

OUR MINDS REVEAL OUR HEARTS

IDENTIFY

○ Where does your mind wander when you have free time?

○ What concerns, fears, or lies typically run through your head throughout the day?

● THINK ABOUT THE THINGS that keep your mind running at night and where your mind wanders during the day. On this fallen earth so full of concerns and cares and tasks, it is too easy to have our minds fixated on the demands of this life. It is not hard for our thoughts to become cluttered with a hundred different tasks, concerns, and daydreams instead of being colored by the secure hope laid up for us in heaven (1 Peter 1:3–5).

Our thoughts will soon dictate our beliefs and actions. The apostle Paul was aware of this pervasive human struggle and reminded the Colossians in the first century that what our minds meditate upon matters. They too struggled with staying focused on the most important things when surrounded by concerns and desires that seemed urgent. Thus, he reminds them that the most significant thing about them was that their lives were hidden with Christ in God (Colossians 3:3). If Christ is the most significant person in their lives, and, if Christ is seated at the right hand of

IF THEN YOU HAVE BEEN RAISED WITH CHRIST, SEEK THE THINGS THAT ARE ABOVE, WHERE CHRIST IS, SEATED AT THE RIGHT HAND OF GOD. SET YOUR MINDS ON THINGS THAT ARE ABOVE, NOT ON THINGS THAT ARE ON EARTH.

COLOSSIANS 3:1-2

the Father in heaven, Paul knows that's where their hearts need to be fixated. If believers are not intentionally keeping their hearts fixed on the truth—the things that are above—they will naturally drift away from Christ.

The world has its own varied versions of meditation and affirmations, but Christian meditation centers not on self or positivity but on the very person and work of Jesus Christ. Christian meditation is more than mere wishful thinking or mantras; it is a constant recalling to our minds that Christ is our very life.

Christian meditation takes practice and awareness. When our minds wander to worries or fears or lies, we must gently lead them back to the truths of the gospel. In fact, we will find ourselves having to do this countless times every hour. Just like untended gardens quickly grow weeds but a flourishing garden requires time, attention, and cultivation,

meditating on what is right, true, lovely, and admirable takes intentionality and work (Philippians 4:8–9). Listening to Scripture songs or keeping index cards with favorite verses are small things that help train our hearts and minds to remember big truths!

Paul tells the Colossians to "seek the things that are above" and to "set your minds on things that are above" (Colossians 3:1–2). Both verbs imply an active redirecting of the mind toward God. Left to ourselves, our thoughts will slip earthward and self-ward; however, with the help of the Holy Spirit and the living and active Word of God saturating our hearts, our minds can be lifted to the true reality of whose we are and who the future belongs to (John 16:12–15; Hebrews 4:12–13). When our sights are set on the eternal days before us, the concerns of today are put in right proportion and proper perspective.

- When does your mind most often get caught up in fears, worries, or distractions?

- What habits and practices help you to meditate on God's promises?

- Read Psalm 119:36–37. How do these verses speak into the thought life of a believer?

HOLDING ONTO HOPE TOGETHER

IDENTIFY

○ How would you define hope?

○ What images or phrases come to mind when you think of hope?

● S O M E T I M E S I can be cavalier in my use of the word *hope*. On any given day, I might say all of the following: "I hope my Amazon package arrives in time," "I hope that the weather holds up for the picnic," and "I hope that the cancer diagnosis comes back benign." We use the word *hope* broadly and loosely in our culture, but biblical hope is something far more than an inclination, a wish, or a longing.

For the Christian, hope is both a conviction and an active waiting upon a sure and certain reality. Christian hope is centered in the person of Jesus Christ and upon his return to establish for us a new heaven and a new earth in which righteousness dwells (2 Peter 3:11–13). The apostle Peter reminds us that our hope is a *living* hope absolutely anchored into the person of Jesus Christ (1 Peter 1:3–5). While all other lesser hopes attached to created things will eventually fade and die, hope centered on the person of the resurrected Christ will be fulfilled.

LET US HOLD FAST THE CONFESSION OF OUR HOPE WITHOUT WAVERING, FOR HE WHO PROMISED IS FAITHFUL. AND LET US CONSIDER HOW TO STIR UP ONE ANOTHER TO LOVE AND GOOD WORKS, NOT NEGLECTING TO MEET TOGETHER, AS IS THE HABIT OF SOME, BUT ENCOURAGING ONE ANOTHER, AND ALL THE MORE AS YOU SEE THE DAY DRAWING NEAR.

HEBREWS 10:23-25

The writer of Hebrews paints a helpful word picture of an anchor line when speaking to the early church about the power of hope in God: "We have this as a pure and steadfast anchor of the soul" (Hebrews 6:19). By using the Greek word *katecho*, he challenges the Hebrew believers to cling to, to bind themselves to, and to take possession of the hope stored up for them by their Savior (Hebrews 10:23). You can't grab onto a whim or a dream—you can only hold on to an actual reality.

Notice the corporate, communal language around holding on to hope: "Let us hold fast the confession of our hope" and "Let us consider how to stir up one another to love and good works" (vv. 23–24). If we are to live hopeful, secure lives in a broken, insecure world, we will need to remind one another of the unshakeable realities our lives are built upon. When my faith begins to falter, I need friends who hold my tired hands to the anchor line of Jesus and his unshakeable kingdom. You do too.

We continually gather as believers because we daily need to be reminded that our hope is certain and centered on Jesus (v. 25). Our all-sufficient Savior enables us to live with security and certainty even in the most trying of circumstances. We are anchored together until the day when hope becomes fulfillment and faith becomes sight.

CONSIDER

- What is the difference between biblical hope and hope as the world defines it?

- Where and when are you tempted to let go of the anchor line of hope?

- Read Romans 5:1–5. What do these verses tell us about our hope as believers?

TAKE + SHARE

The world is constantly telling us we are not enough and we don't have enough. This scarcity mindset bleeds into our spiritual lives. We forget that Jesus will always be enough for his people. Identify places in your life and around you where you are living out of a scarcity mindset. Remember that our God is a God of abundance. Consider memorizing Psalm 130:7, which proclaims: "O Israel, hope in the LORD! For with the LORD there is steadfast love, and with him is plentiful redemption."

As you reflect on the generosity of God toward you, look for areas of need in the lives of those around you. Prayerfully consider how you might seek to meet one or more of these needs out of the abundance God has given you. Maybe you can babysit for a single parent or make a meal for a struggling friend! The possibilities are as endless as the needs!

When we find our security and identity in Christ, we are freed to live differently than the watching world. Contrary to popular belief, theology is not a mere cerebral affair; rather, what we believe plays itself out practically in our daily lives: in our families, at our places of work, and in our communities. This week we will explore the practical realities of security in Christ!

LIVING SECURELY IN CHRIST

THE GLORY TO COME

IDENTIFY

○ How often do you think about heaven?

○ What do you find most compelling and comforting when you think of heaven?

● HAVE YOUR FRIENDS ever spoiled a movie for you? I know mine most certainly have. Watching a movie and already knowing the end is a completely different experience from watching it blindly. Even though the tension still exists and we feel anxiety as the climax builds, when we know how the story ends, we experience the story differently.

As silly as it sounds, the apostle Paul offers a biblical spoiler to the Colossians (and to us). He reminds us that we already know how the story ends: Christ will return to establish a new heaven and a new earth wherein we will be forever with God (2 Peter 3:11–13; Revelation 21:1–4). He reminds us that our very lives are securely hidden with Christ in God and that when Christ ushers in glory, we will be with him (Colossians 3:3–4).

Knowing the beautiful end of our earthly stories changes the way we experience the messy middle. If this earthly life is all we have, it is understandable to approach it with the prevailing

FOR YOU HAVE DIED, AND YOUR LIFE IS HIDDEN WITH CHRIST IN GOD. WHEN CHRIST WHO IS YOUR LIFE APPEARS, THEN YOU ALSO WILL APPEAR WITH HIM IN GLORY.

COLOSSIANS 3:3-4

cultural notion of YOLO (you only live once). If, however, we rightly understand the glories that await us in the presence of God, we will live in such a way that the watching world will wonder at the hope within us (1 Peter 3:15).

We can better endure tears and trials knowing that one day he will dry every tear from our eyes (Revelation 21:4). We can bear up under the weight of suffering knowing that our sufferings are not worth comparing to the eternal weight of glory we will experience (2 Corinthians 4:16–18). We can forego earthly accolades and applause knowing that one day we will hear the Father's proud, "Well done, good and faithful servant" (Matthew 25:21). Our todays are nothing compared to the coming Day when God will usher in endless days.

Cancer, loneliness, singleness, infertility, or any other number of hardships do not have the last word in the life of a believer; God does. And the end is sure.

- What present realities threaten to steal your attention from future glory?

- When is the last time you found yourself thinking of the glories of the new heavens and the new earth?

- Read 1 John 3:1–3. What do these verses tell us about our future as believers?

PUTTING OFF AND PUTTING ON

IDENTIFY

○ What habits in your daily life do you need to lay aside to experience more of Jesus?

○ What habits in your daily life do you want to put on to experience more of Jesus?

WHEN WE PURCHASED our first home in San Diego, we were simultaneously relieved and anxious. We were thrilled to have a home with "good bones" and great potential; however, as we looked at the amount of demolition it would take to get closer to our dream home, we were terribly overwhelmed. Before we could paint walls and hang up pictures, we had to tear down existing walls that were structurally unsound. We had to tear down before we could build up.

Paul uses a similar analogy to help the Colossians understand the path toward continued growth as a believer: the language of putting off and putting on. We must put off the old self continually so that we might live out of the new self. This language of our sinful natures as the flesh, the old man, and the old nature shows up throughout the entire New Testament.

Paul encouraged the early believers to "put off your old self, which belongs to your former manner of life and is corrupt

DO NOT LIE TO ONE ANOTHER, SEEING THAT YOU HAVE PUT OFF THE OLD SELF WITH ITS PRACTICES AND HAVE PUT ON THE NEW SELF, WHICH IS BEING RENEWED IN KNOWLEDGE AFTER THE IMAGE OF ITS CREATOR.

COLOSSIANS 3:9-10

through deceitful desires, and to be renewed in the spirit of your minds, and to put on the new self, created after the likeness of God in true righteousness and holiness" (Ephesians 4:22–24).

Before we can grow into the cloaks of righteousness Christ procured for us, the worn-out garments of our old selves need to be exposed, named, and removed through repentance. We must put off before we can put on. Christ exposes our anger, evil desires, malice, and falsehood so that he might clothe us in the fruit of the gospel: kindness, compassion, and forgiveness (more on this tomorrow). While this disrobing of sin happens initially in salvation, it continues to happen in an ongoing way in the process of sanctification. We must continue this process of putting off and putting on until the day when we will no longer have an indwelling sinful nature warring against our truest, deepest identity in Christ (Galatians 5:16–26).

● When talking about what we need to put off, Paul offers the Colossians two sample lists (Colossians 3:5, 9). What do you notice about these two lists? Which of these sins do you most often struggle with?

● What old patterns of the old self are hard to put off? Why do you think this is so?

● When Christ exposes your old self, he always dresses you in his promises. What promises of God can you claim for your life today?

PUT ON LOVE

IDENTIFY

○ When others describe you,
what words do they most often use?

○ When you think of what you want to
define you, what words would you use?

● SILLY CONFESSION: one time I was trying on a cute, Boho top in a Target dressing room and got completely stuck in said shirt. When I say stuck, I mean a stuck that induced sweat and a near panic attack. Embarrassed, I had to ask another person in the fitting room for help in getting out of the mess I had made. Clearly, I should have tried on the next size up.

While I share this in jest, this story also offers us perspective when we are reading Paul's invitation to put off the old man to make room for the new. Often, we struggle with divesting ourselves of our old sinful ways because we try to do it alone and in our own strength. No wonder we often find ourselves as spiritually discouraged and tangled as I was in the dressing room.

Whatever God commands, he also enables and empowers (2 Peter 1:3). God stands ready to help us in our spiritual dressing rooms, fitting us with new garments of patience, forgiveness, and love toward each other. Here's the really exciting truth: the more comfortable we become in receiving the love that God has for us, the more we will become like Christ in reflecting his compassion, kindness, forgiveness, and peace in our relationships.

For the believer, all things flow from the central reality of the love of Christ. We love only because he first loved us (1 John 4:19). As we abide in his love, we will obey his commandments (John 15:9–10). The more we learn to wear the love of Christ as our cloak, the more our lives will be marked by the fruits of the Spirit. The marks of the old self (impurity, covetousness, idolatry, malice, anger, etc.) will be replaced by the peace of Christ which will act like a referee in our hearts, bringing order and security in our souls (Colossians 3:15).

Imagine what could happen in your relationships and in your community if you and fellow believers around you consistently lived this way. This is the picture Jesus gave us in John 13:35: "By this all people will know that you are my disciples, if you have love for one another."

PUT ON THEN, AS GOD'S CHOSEN ONES, HOLY AND BELOVED, COMPASSIONATE HEARTS, KINDNESS, HUMILITY, MEEKNESS, AND PATIENCE, BEARING WITH ONE ANOTHER AND, IF ONE HAS A COMPLAINT AGAINST ANOTHER, FORGIVING EACH OTHER, AS THE LORD HAS FORGIVEN YOU, SO YOU ALSO MUST FORGIVE. AND ABOVE ALL THESE PUT ON LOVE, WHICH BINDS EVERYTHING TOGETHER IN PERFECT HARMONY.

COLOSSIANS 3:12–14

FOR THE BELIEVER,

ALL THINGS FLOW

FROM THE CENTRAL

REALITY OF THE

LOVE OF CHRIST. WE

LOVE ONLY BECAUSE

HE FIRST LOVED US.

CONSIDER

- Compare Paul's list here (Colossians 3:12) with a similar list of spiritual fruit in Galatians 5:22–24. What do you notice? What stands out to you?

- Is there anyone you have been struggling to forgive? If so, pray for God to remind you of all the forgiveness you have received from him.

- How can you practically show compassion and love to those in your immediate circles this week?

GOD'S PLAN FOR SECURE FAMILIES

IDENTIFY

○ What are some of the gifts
God gives us through family?

○ What are some of the challenges
you experience within your family?

WHILE FEW HAVE TRUDGED through the entirety of Leo Tolstoy's masterpiece *Anna Karenina*, many are familiar with its opening line: "All happy families are more or less like one another; every unhappy family is unhappy in its own particular way."[2]

Even those who haven't read this famous line likely resonate with its meaning. We all know how formative our experiences of family can be, whether for good or ill. Few influences leave such a lasting mark on our lives and personalities as our families of origin. The New Testament writers understood the significance of the family. As such, they addressed how the gospel changes the way we live as families.

While these verses in chapter 3 may sound jarring in our present age, they are time-tested principles for the thriving of the most basic unit of society. In an age when women and children were considered less-than and not formally addressed as entities, Paul offers unique commands to both husbands and wives,

WIVES, SUBMIT TO YOUR HUSBANDS, AS IS FITTING IN THE LORD. HUSBANDS, LOVE YOUR WIVES, AND DO NOT BE HARSH WITH THEM. CHILDREN, OBEY YOUR PARENTS IN EVERYTHING, FOR THIS PLEASES THE LORD. FATHERS, DO NOT PROVOKE YOUR CHILDREN, LEST THEY BECOME DISCOURAGED.

COLOSSIANS 3:18–21

parents and children. Each part of the family is called to unique ways of relating to one another to ensure that the family works well and has its own structural integrity.

Because Christ is all and in all (Colossians 3:11), Christ must be the center of the family. Thus, husbands are neither to abnegate nor abuse power, but rather to use their role as heads of the family to serve and protect the family. Wives are to trust the Lord by trusting the stable structures he has set in order. Parents are not to lord over their children but to be thoughtful and gentle in rearing them. Children are to honor their parents as the authorities that God has loving set over them for their good. Everyone has a part to play,

each different but each equally challenging to the flesh.

For families to provide the intended support and nourishment God designed them to provide, Christ must be at the center of the family. His commands are for our good and the flourishing of our families, even when they challenge our flesh or push us out of our comfort zones.

The gospel changes everything, not the least the way we approach living as families. Those whose families modeled biblical principles know that such a reality was the gift of grace, while those with less-than-ideal family experiences are invited to healing experiences within the family of God.

- What uncertainties have filled your mind when you think about submission? What strikes you about this arrangement for the Christian family?

- How does Colossians 3:12–15 give you a way forward when you think about marriage? How does putting on love bring unity?

- In Ephesians 5:22–33 Paul talks more in-depth about Christian marriage. What is the underlying motivation behind the unique commands to husbands and wives?

- God teaches us what he is like as a father through both comparison and contrast to our earthly fathers. What was your experience with your earthly father?

THE PRISON OF PEOPLE-PLEASING

IDENTIFY

○ Whose approval do you long for and work for?

○ What does your work ethic reveal about your heart?

DO YOU REMEMBER your first job and all the excitement, earnestness, and nervousness you brought to those early weeks of work? Every time I drive by an Applebee's restaurant, I remember anew all the feelings of adolescent employment.

After the excitement of a job wears off, however, it's easy to lose sight of why and for whom we are ultimately working. This is true for any task on our plates, whether or not it is paid work. It can easily degrade into people-pleasing or drudgery. When the applause of people compels our work, we will burn ourselves out and eventually lose heart. When it feels like drudgery, work feels like a dead end that's going nowhere.

Paul helps us to see that no matter our context, any work we are given to do is an opportunity to work for the glory of God. When God sees the heart behind what we are doing, any work can become worship. This is true whether we are a CEO of a Fortune 500 company or whether we are cleaning bathrooms.

WHATEVER YOU DO, WORK HEARTILY, AS FOR THE LORD AND NOT FOR MEN, KNOWING THAT FROM THE LORD YOU WILL RECEIVE THE INHERITANCE AS YOUR REWARD. YOU ARE SERVING THE LORD CHRIST.

COLOSSIANS 3:23-24

When Paul addresses slaves and masters, he speaks out of the Roman practice where people could temporarily and voluntarily put themselves in servitude to pay off a debt. Rather than debate the cultural practices of his day, Paul addresses the hearts of both masters and slaves, bosses, and subordinates.[3]

Both servant and boss are called to live out their positions under the lordship of Christ. Those under authority are to remember that their end goal is to please the Lord, not a human overseer or boss. Those in positions of authority are to remember that they, too, have a master in the Lord. They will be held accountable for their treatment of those under their authority.

The heart of work as a Christian is to serve the Lord as the ultimate supervisor who sees all. We are invited to leave the prison of people-pleasing for the freedom of serving a good God. We need not grow weary in doing good (Galatians 6:7–9). We need not grow bitter if our bosses or constituents don't recognize or appreciate our work. Our God sees and he will reward us without partiality (Colossians 3:25).

Rather than chasing the fickle approval of others, we are invited to glorify God in our work because we have a fixed approval of Christ. From this solid foundation, we are free to serve others without expecting them to meet our needs. When we live in his pleasure, we are freed from the prison of man's approval!

CONSIDER

- What people do you tend to want to please most? When do you most often slip into people-pleasing?

- Whatever your current work situation, what is the present condition of your heart toward your work?

- What practically helps you remember your true, Good Master throughout your workdays?

TAKE + SHARE

What we truly believe will eventually show up in our lives in practical ways. When we hold fast to Christ and find our security in him, we are freed to live differently in this world. We can sincerely love and serve others and lay down our need for the approval of man. This week, ask the Lord for specific ways you can serve in the spheres of family and work. Look for specific ways you can bless without expecting anything in return, knowing the security and approval you already have in Jesus!

W **8**

Our security in Christ is a communal affair. We won't last long or get very far in our walks with God apart from the encouragement of a gospel community. This week we will more deeply explore the significant role community plays in our perseverance in the gospel.

SECURE TOGETHER

A POSTURE OF PRAYER

IDENTIFY

○ How often do you ask others to pray for you?

○ What do you pray for your loved ones?

● YOU CAN LEARN about the nature of my relationship with my husband by looking at our text thread history. You'd see affectionate texts (Love you, babe!), informational texts (I'll be ten minutes late), and requests for help (Can you pick up the boys?). The varied nature of our conversations would show you a lived-in love with varied communication.

The same is true of our prayer lives. They reveal the nature of our relationship with God. We can learn much about the present condition of our relationship with God through examining the trends in our times of prayer. Whom do we pray for? What do we ask for most desperately?

Paul bookends his letter to the Colossians with prayer. He began this short letter by praying for the Colossians, and he begins his conclusion inviting them to pray for him. Paul models that prayer is not an event in the day of the believer's life; rather, it is the believer's lifeline. Prayer is not simply a part of the

CONTINUE STEADFASTLY IN PRAYER, BEING WATCHFUL IN IT WITH THANKSGIVING.

COLOSSIANS 4:2

believer's daily schedule; it is the posture of the Christian life.

As Paul is writing this letter, he is literally sitting in prison. If I were in prison and someone were to pry into my prayer life, I imagine he would hear me praying desperately for my own concerns (my release being chief among them). However, the glimpse Paul gives us into his prison prayer life shows a man chiefly concerned with the gospel going forth. He wanted open doors for the gospel, not merely open prison doors for himself! He, who found reasons to keep depending upon and praising God even when unjustly imprisoned, exhorts the Colossians to remain steadfast and grateful in their own prayers.

These are not throwaway words to wrap up correspondence—this message is the outworking of a life lived through prayer. In his letter to the Philippians, we learn that Paul did not consider prayer a divine vending machine to get that which he wanted from God. He had learned the secret of being content in all circumstances: God is both gift and giver (Philippians 4:10–13). Paul always found reasons to prayerfully rejoice. He was constantly bringing his anxieties, concerns, and cares before God because he knew how deeply God cared about him (Philippians 4:4–7).

Prayer is both spontaneous and structured, individual and communal, work and worship. Prayer is our ongoing conversation and connection with the God who made us, loves us, and shows deep concern for our everyday experiences. The heart of prayer is bringing all of who we are and where we really are (not where we *ought* to be) to God. In prayer, we don't seek to shape God's will to fit ours, rather, we invite God to shape our wills to his.

CONSIDER

- If someone listened in to your prayer life, what would it say about your relationship with God and your priorities?

- Sometimes we make prayer more complicated than it needs to be. Read Jesus's model for prayer in Luke 11:1–4. What strikes you as you read this prayer?

- A good way to jump-start stalled-out prayer lives is to ask God to search our hearts. Read and pray Psalm 139:23–24.

AN OUTWARD-FACING HEART

IDENTIFY

○ Do you remember a time when you were an outsider?

○ How did it feel?

○ What outsiders has God placed around you?

AS SOMEONE WHO did not grow up in the church, I distinctly remember how it felt to walk into church with no knowledge, no experience, and no clue what was happening all around me. Thankfully, I wasn't shamed or excluded; rather, I was gently and winsomely invited into a new family. I access these memories all the time when I interact with the "outsiders" in my life: the refugee families I've had the opportunity to befriend, the friends who recently moved into town, and the high schoolers who don't quite know where they belong.

God has an undeniable heart for the outsider, the alien, and the stranger. God's people were to invite the aliens and outsiders among them into Sabbath rest (Exodus 20:8–11). God's people were commanded to not exploit strangers or outsiders (22:21–24). The Lord continually sought to remind his people that they themselves knew how it felt to be sojourners, outsiders, and strangers (23:9; Deuteronomy 10:19).

WALK IN WISDOM TOWARD OUTSIDERS, MAKING THE BEST USE OF THE TIME. LET YOUR SPEECH ALWAYS BE GRACIOUS, SEASONED WITH SALT, SO THAT YOU MAY KNOW HOW YOU OUGHT TO ANSWER EACH PERSON.

COLOSSIANS 4:5-6

Thus, it should not be surprising to us that Jesus both lived and proclaimed the exact same stance toward those outside of the promises of God. After a long day of healing and serving in multiple cities, Jesus's heart toward the outsiders did not wane. According to the disciples who were with him, "When he saw the crowds, he had compassion for them, because they were harassed and helpless, like sheep without a shepherd" (Matthew 9:36). Similarly, Jesus was quick to love the outsiders and invite them into fellowship with him, whether they be Samaritans, sinners, lepers, or those otherwise cast off from society (Matthew 8:1–4; Luke 5:27–32; John 4).

If our triune God is aware of and concerned for outsiders, our lives should show a similar care and concern. In his closing remarks to the Colossians, Paul includes some insights into how to approach and live among those who are outside the faith: with words of grace and thoughtfulness.

The first step toward loving the outsider is asking God to help you truly see them. Ask God to open your eyes to the strangers and the outsiders and to give you his eyes to see them as he sees them. Empathetic curiosity goes a long way in the kingdom of God. Ask good questions of those around you. Hear what is important to them. Seek to learn their stories. Your love and graciousness may give you an open door to share your own story with them.

CONSIDER

- Read 1 Peter 3:14–17. What does Peter have to say about our stance toward outsiders to the faith?

- Who are some of the outsiders God has placed in your life? What is your heart attitude toward them?

- What specific verses can you pray for these people who may be close to you but far from God?

A BAND OF BROTHERS + SISTERS

IDENTIFY

○ Is there an area in your life where you
are experiencing loneliness?

○ When is the last time you felt closely
partnered with someone in the family of God?

● A S A M O T H E R of three active boys, I have nearly mastered
the art of speed-reading or not-reading waivers, permission slips,
and other long forms. My mind hears "Yadah, yadah, yadah" when
I see those long lists and see all the legal verbiage. Unfortunately,
our minds can slip into a similar semi-reading mode at the beginning and end of the epistles (letters) that make up a large portion
of the New Testament. However, far from being throwaway por-
tions of the letters to the early churches, the beginnings and ends
ground these heartfelt letters in an historic network of real
relationships.

Paul knew firsthand the realities of life with real people in real
circumstances in the real world. He understood that the greatest
joys and the greatest sorrows we experience in life are relational.
He did not merely preach the absolute necessity of community to
a well-lived life as a follower of Jesus; he lived it.

As he closes his letter to the Colossians, Paul mentions eight

TYCHICUS WILL TELL YOU ALL ABOUT MY ACTIVITIES. HE IS A BELOVED BROTHER AND FAITHFUL MINISTER AND FELLOW SERVANT IN THE LORD. I HAVE SENT HIM TO YOU FOR THIS VERY PURPOSE, THAT YOU MAY KNOW HOW WE ARE AND THAT HE MAY ENCOURAGE YOUR HEARTS.

COLOSSIANS 4:7-8

coworkers and friends in his work of spreading the gospel to the known world. Rather than gloss over these names as insignificant to us, we are invited to double down on each name mentioned. From this network of names, we get a glimpse into the band of brothers and sisters who did life with Paul and the other apostles. Having been with Jesus as a band of brothers for three years and having been sent out two by two by him (Luke 9:1–2), the original disciples had ingrained in them the significance of community and team ministry.

The more mature we become, the more we also learn to lean into gospel community. This does not mean relationships happen easily, however. Particularly in our individualistic society, we have to be very intentional to invite others into the rhythms of our daily life and to take the risk of sharing our lives and our burdens with them.

It can be slow, messy, and imperfect, but the reality is that we simply were not meant to live life on our own. We won't make it very far in the life of faith in isolation. We are made in the image of a triune God who exists in relationship within himself; thus, we were created for relationships and partnership. If you are experiencing loneliness or isolation, bring those emotions into the presence of God and ask him to provide a band of brothers and sisters!

IT CAN BE SLOW,

MESSY, AND

IMPERFECT, BUT

THE REALITY IS

THAT WE SIMPLY

WERE NOT MEANT

TO LIVE LIFE ON

OUR OWN.

CONSIDER

- Who has been an Epaphras in your life (praying and encouraging you toward maturity)? To whom is God calling you to be an Epaphras?

- Are there any places where you are experiencing loneliness in life or ministry? If not, thank God for his gracious provisions of a network of relationships. If not, spend time bringing your needs and desires for a stronger relational network before God.

- Are there any people God might be calling you to step toward with intentionality?

MATURITY TAKES A TEAM

IDENTIFY

○ Who has helped you grow in your relationship with Christ?

○ How has God recently been making you more mature in your faith?

WHEN WE MOVED to Southern California over twelve years ago, we were blown away by the fresh citrus fruit available everywhere: on roadsides, from neighbors, at local farmer's markets. We decided to take advantage of the favorable climate and plant our own blood orange tree.

That tiny sapling required a disproportionate amount of care from me: twice daily watering until it became established and an hour of weekly watering thereafter. I watched YouTube videos on pruning and everything. It took some years before our little tree began bearing enough fruit for our family of five to enjoy. But, let me tell you, no fruit ever tasted so amazing—not because the store fruits were not tasty, but because of the effort and toil and care I poured into this plant.

If helping a plant on toward maturity offers such joy, imagine the joy of struggling and working alongside a soul that is moving toward fullness and maturity in Christ. As an aged man who was

EPAPHRAS, WHO IS ONE OF YOU, A SERVANT OF CHRIST JESUS, GREETS YOU, ALWAYS STRUGGLING ON YOUR BEHALF IN HIS PRAYERS, THAT YOU MAY STAND MATURE AND FULLY ASSURED IN ALL THE WILL OF GOD. FOR I BEAR HIM WITNESS THAT HE HAS WORKED HARD FOR YOU AND FOR THOSE IN LAODICEA AND IN HIERAPOLIS.

COLOSSIANS 4:12-13

an exile on the island of Patmos and writing to the young churches, the apostle John shared, "I have no greater joy than to hear that my children are walking in the truth" (3 John 1:4). Those are strong words from a man who knew the joy of living for three years alongside Jesus. Those who know the peace, love, and joy of being in relationship with Christ long that their loved ones would experience the same.

As he wraps up his letter to the Colossians, Paul specifically mentions Epaphras, a man who loved the Lord and who worked and prayed hard to see his local church established and mature. While he likely had many other identifiers, Paul helps us see that Epaphras's deepest identity was being a servant of the Lord. Not only that, but his great ambition was to see others "stand mature and fully assured in all the will of God" (Colossians 4:12). In a world marked by insecurity and immaturity, Epaphras labored to see the Colossians fully secure in Christ.

We don't reach maturity easily and without effort—our own effort and the efforts of those who labor on our behalf in teaching, prayer, fellowship, and acts of service. We need others to encourage us when we waver, and we need to do the same for them. Thankfully, God is the great gardener: everything he plants, he will cause to flourish. Everything he begins, he carries through to completion (Philippians 1:6).

CONSIDER

● Where are you presently struggling to stand "fully assured in all the will of God"?

● Read Psalm 18:27–30. What do we learn about the will of God in these verses?

RUN YOUR RACE

IDENTIFY

○ What are some of the specific callings on your life?

○ What unique gifts and experiences might
God be inviting you to steward for the kingdom of God?

● AS I MENTIONED EARLIER, I used to run marathons (emphasis on the phrase "used to"). There were moments of misery and long stretches of pain and doubt in each race, but all of these faded away the moment my feet crossed the finish line. The finishing makes all the hardships and sacrifices of training well worth it!

The apostle Paul often used the analogy of running a race when he described the Christian life. Each believer has a course marked out for him or her by God himself (Hebrews 12:1–2). Each believer is uniquely wired by God for specific good works that God has planned for them to walk into (Ephesians 2:8–10). Luke wrote the gospel of Luke and Acts (Colossians 4:14). Nympha hosted a church in her house (Colossians 4:15). Both ministries were significant. Each believer is called to run their course to completion through the strength that God provides (Acts 20:24). As he was facing impending death, Paul expresses to Timothy relief and celebration at having run his race well to the end: "I have fought

LUKE THE BELOVED PHYSICIAN GREETS YOU, AS DOES DEMAS. GIVE MY GREETINGS TO THE BROTHERS AT LAODICEA, AND TO NYMPHA AND THE CHURCH IN HER HOUSE. AND WHEN THIS LETTER HAS BEEN READ AMONG YOU, HAVE IT ALSO READ IN THE CHURCH OF THE LAODICEANS; AND SEE THAT YOU ALSO READ THE LETTER FROM LAODICEA.

COLOSSIANS 4:14-16

the good fight, I have finished the race, I have kept the faith" (2 Timothy 4:7).

Nestled in the end of Paul's letter to the Colossians is a list of names which initially seem irrelevant to us. However, these names remind us that the kingdom comes through an entire ensemble of faithful followers. Our choices matter. Our unseen acts of service and faith and forgiveness matter. Even if no one names a building after us, our God sees, hears, and knows our lives. When we are tempted to despair or defeat, we are invited to take Paul's words to heart, "And let us not grow weary of doing good, for in due season we will reap, if we do not give up" (Galatians 6:9).

Each of our races is different, as were Paul's and Timothy's; however, Paul's encouragement to Archippus to "See that you fulfill the ministry that you have received in the Lord" applies to us equally (Colossians 4:17). We each have a role to play in the advancement of the kingdom of God. Our courses matter, and our constant companion, the Holy Spirit, encourages us to keep running.

● What do you sense God has called you to do in this season to work for the advancement of the kingdom?

● Where and when are you most tempted to grow weary while doing good?

● Read Hebrews 12:12–14. What encouragement do we find here for those who are weary?

TAKE + SHARE

Paul closes his letter simultaneously high up in the heavens (through prayer) and with two feet on the ground (within a network of relationships). Both are essential parts to the Christian life. Reach out to your relational network this week, not only to ask for prayer for yourself but also to ask for their prayer requests. Think of one person who has helped you run your race and one person who seems tempted to give up on theirs. Spend time praying specifically for them and consider writing them a note of thanks or encouragement.

ACKNOWLEDGMENTS

THE MORE I WRITE, the more I realize that writing truly is a team effort. I am deeply grateful to the Lord from whom we receive every good gift (James 1:17). And gifts are replete in this project. My husband, G'Joe, and my three sons, Tyus, Eli, and Phin, graciously offered the gifts of time and space to focus on writing. The women of Redeemer Presbyterian Church in Encinitas, California gave me the gift of time spent studying the book of Colossians together. The body of Christ at Center City Church in La Mesa, California, offered the gifts of prayer and encouragement throughout this project. The team at New Growth Press gave me the opportunity to write for this series, which I consider an incredible gift. Ruth, Barbara, and Amanda gave me the gift of excellent editorial work. God has been lavish in his grace toward me in the process of working on this devotional. I pray he shows the same lavish grace to you through this work.

ENDNOTES

[1] Alexis de Tocqueville, *Democracy in America* (New York: Bantam Books, 2002), 659.

[2] Leo Tolstoy, *Anna Karenina* (Switzerland: Heron Books, 1958), 1.

[3] Due to limited space and the scope of this devotional, there is not ample space to go into detail on this significant topic. If you are interested in further discussion around the topic of slavery in the Scriptures, the following is a helpful starting point: Sam Storms, "10 Things You Should Know about Slavery in the Bible," Sam Storms Enjoying God blog, February 18, 2019, *https://www.samstorms.org/enjoying-god-blog/post/10-things-you-should-know-about-slavery-in-the-bible*.

ENDORSEMENTS

"In our culture today, identity is a hot topic. People are taught to find their identity in how they feel, what they do, or what they have. But the Bible teaches otherwise. In Aimee Joseph's devotional, *You Are Secure*, readers are invited to learn from the book of Colossians. These rich, accessible devotions draw us into the heart of the gospel. Aimee is a friendly and gracious guide, walking us through the chapters of Paul's letter, pointing us to an identity that is solid and secure. It's not found in what we feel, what job we do, or what we desire; it is found in our union with Christ alone."

Christina Fox, Speaker; author of *Who Are You? A Little Book About Your Big Identity*

"Finding our gospel footing in an anxious and unstable world can often be difficult. Aimee Joseph's new devotional encourages the reader to divert their thoughts from their temporal concerns to set their minds on the things that are above. The visually engaging format and the accessible length are ideal for readers."

Karen Hodge, Coordinator of Women's Ministries, Presbyterian Church in America (PCA); author of *Transformed: Life-taker to Life-giver* and *Life-giving Leadership*

"Behold and belong! While the world is distracting and being distracted to death, Aimee Joseph shows us how to be planted securely in our life in Christ. *You Are Secure* helps us ponder important questions about our identity and the relationships that define us. You are loved with an everlasting love, and you are held in God's everlasting arms."

Irene Sun, Bible teacher; author of *God Counts* and *Taste and See*

"The paradoxical message of our fallen world is that you are enough and yet you don't have enough. Colossians encourages us with the timeless truth that only Jesus Christ is enough, and he is for us. In this insightful and illuminating study, Aimee Joseph unpacks truths that have anchored and stabilized weary Christian sojourners for two millennia."

Beverly Berrus, Author; Bible teacher; pastor's wife

"As we make our way through life in a world with so much uncertainty about the future, we need a daily touchstone, a daily tethering to the source of our hope, which is exactly what Aimee Joseph provides in *You Are Secure*. Each day's brief insights into Scripture and penetrating application questions help to keep Christ at the center of our thoughts, our conversations, and our confidence."

Nancy Guthrie, Author; Bible teacher

"Colossians is a small but powerful book. In this eight-week Bible study, Aimee Joseph serves as a skillful guide. Each day's reading feels like opening the Scriptures with a friend who helps us not only go deeper in our study but also to allow God's Word to permeate our thoughts, emotions, and perceptions about who he is and what he's doing in our lives. This two-month journey will serve well those who are brand new to Christianity, as well as those who have been walking with Jesus for decades. I'm grateful for this new resource for the church."

Jen Oshman, Author; podcast host; women's ministry director

"Aimee Joseph soaks herself in Scripture. In *You Are Secure*, she reminds us of the width, depth, and breadth of God's love and how our identities and lives find security only in Christ. Exploring Colossians, this devotional firmly, gently, and practically reminds readers that union with Christ is the aim of our churches and lives."

Ashley Hales, Author of *A Spacious Life*; cofounder, The Willowbrae Institute